# IF ONLY
# I HAD SAID . . .

# IF ONLY
# I HAD SAID . . .

*Conversation Control Skills
for Managers*

## CHARLES J. MARGERISON

**MERCURY**

First published in 1987
as *Conversation Control Skills for Managers*
by the Mercury Books Division of
W. H. Allen & Co. Plc
Sekforde House, 175–9 St John Street,
London EC1V 4LL

Reprinted 1987 (twice)
Published in paperback 1990

Set in Concorde by Phoenix Photosetting
Printed and bound in Great Britain by
Mackays of Chatham PLC, Chatham, Kent

*British Library Cataloguing in Publication Data*

Margerison, Charles J.
   Conversation control skills for managers.
   1. Conversation      2. Communication in
   management
   I. Title
   808.56'024658       P95.45

   ISBN 1 85252 012 4

To
Colinette
*for*
*21 of the best years*

# Contents

# Introduction

What you say and how you say it are two keys to success, particularly when you are in a managerial position, accountable for getting a team of people to work together, and influencing other colleagues. Knowing how to control your own conversation is a major step in developing more effective managerial performance. As Rudyard Kipling said, 'Words are the most powerful drug used by mankind'. So we need to use them with care.

In this book I have put together the main points that you need to concentrate upon in order to improve your conversation control skills. The principles have been well tested in practice by the many managers and advisers I have taught on various workshops. The examples I draw upon come from the world of engineering, sales, auditing, personnel, administration and other aspects of managerial life.

My interest in the influence conversational skill has in management and social life was developed considerably by Professor Norman Maier and I value those contributions as reflected in this book.

I appreciate the support of Anne Dombrovskis, who has expertly managed the word processing of the manuscript, and Jane Aberle, who has completed the final version. Special thanks are due to Jim Kable for his well directed advice and interest in the work, and to Rod Davies, Dick McCann, and Marilyn Rafter.

The book reflects the support and encouragement of my wife Colinette, who has provided the important home conditions necessary for me to complete this work. The motivation to complete the book came from my four children – Jill, Alan, Colinette and John.

*Charles J. Margerison*, 1987

CHAPTER ONE

# How to Assess Your Conversation Control

'When *I* use a word,' Humpty Dumpty said in a rather scornful tone, 'it means just what I choose it to mean, – neither more nor less.'

'The question is,' said Alice, 'whether you *can* make words mean different things.'

'The question is,' said Humpty Dumpty, 'which is to be master – that's all.'

Lewis Carroll: *Alice through the Looking Glass*

---

To get things done as a manager you have to influence others. A key skill is your use of conversation control – what you say and how you say it. People who are successful are usually skilled in conversational control, but few people understand the principles behind it. Managing a conversation is a skill and in this chapter we shall cover:

- the meaning of conversation control
- a self-assessment of your skills
- the benefits of conversation control
- areas for application and use

---

You can improve your conversation control skills and be more effective in interviews, meetings, and negotiations, as well as socially more at ease. We shall examine specific cases and examples which you can use as a basis for improving the way you communicate.

## What is Conversation Control?

Years ago La Rochefoucauld in his *Maxims* stated: 'To listen closely and reply well is the highest perfection we are able to attain in the art of conversation'.

Let us say right at the outset that conversation control does not mean that you can control someone else's conversation. What it does mean is that with practice you can control your own conversation, and in time be able to influence others and encourage them to respond in a positive and relevant way.

We shall deal with the words used and the way we use them. For example, the tone that we use in conversation can make or break what we say. It can be sharp and aggressive or measured and reasonable. Likewise the timing of what we say can have a major impact.

How many times have you left a meeting saying 'That was a waste of time', as you walked down the corridor talking to a colleague. I have done it many times and it has reflected not only my own dissatisfaction with the contribution I have made but also dissatisfaction with the level of discussion generally. In short, little was achieved because those attending did not exercise conversation control skills. Equally I have walked out of meetings and said to colleagues 'That was very useful, we achieved a lot there'. Again I can reflect that in such meetings people exercised conversation control skills.

So what are these conversation control skills? They include how to handle personal criticism, how to put forward a proposal, how to register a protest, how to disagree without being aggressive, how to be creative, how to negotiate, how to buy and sell, how to interview and praise, and how to contribute to a meeting. All these seem common activities, but each one of them is central to how we perform our work.

For example, what would you say if the following occurred:

- A subordinate whose work you value asks for an interview and during the meeting says 'I've worked here for three years always doing the same boring job. I have never been invited to go on a training course like many others. Work for me is no longer exciting, it's just routine. Maybe it's time I moved on'. How would you respond?

- You are having a meeting with a colleague at the same organizational level as yourself from the next department. He says to you during the meeting 'I'm continually disappointed that my department does not get enough support and co-operation from your people. I know you say your staff are overworked but I've got people underworked waiting for them to pass on the drawings so we can get moving'. What would be your answer?

2

- Alternatively, your subordinate has just sent you a note saying he does not wish to serve on a working party to assess a new venture. This will mean time away from home. His next promotion could be associated with the new venture, but he does not wish to be away. What would you say?

These are just three examples that could emerge in different forms in your workplace. The words we use and the way we manage the conversations can be critical in the solution of the underlying problem. On other occasions it is not so much a problem we have to deal with but, rather, the seizing of an opportunity. Both problems and opportunities require skilled conversation control.

When you are talking to someone, you soon know if they are able to exercise conversation control. They will listen in a positive way at the right time, yet talk meaningfully when it is their turn. They will know how to change the direction of the conversation without offence. They will move the discussion along at a pleasant pace and build on the key points you raise.

It is easy to observe but difficult to practise. So it is with conversational control. To be successful you need to have guidelines. Such guidelines do not tell us what to say but provide indicators to keep us on track. Throughout this book we shall refer to these guidelines and at the end of each chapter a list will be provided.

Conversation control therefore is a skill. It can be learnt. There are principles to separate poor performance from effective high performance. However, before you proceed, complete the conversation control Personal Assessment Index below. This will give you a quick check of how you see your own skills. From this analysis you can identify where you need to concentrate in order to improve your skills.

## CONVERSATION CONTROL

### Personal Assessment Index

How do you rate your performance on the following aspects of conversation control? Please use the scale shown below to score your personal performance.

# CONVERSATION CONTROL SKILLS FOR MANAGERS

| | Need to improve a lot | Need to improve a bit | Need to practise more | Perform reasonably well | Perform very well |
|---|---|---|---|---|---|
| | 1 | 2 | 3 | 4 | 5 |

| Areas | | Score |
|---|---|---|
| 1. | Summarizing accurately what others say | _____ |
| 2. | Asserting your rights | _____ |
| 3. | Negotiating | _____ |
| 4. | Dealing with differences of opinion | _____ |
| 5. | Getting your message across in conflict situations | _____ |
| 6. | Finding out what other people think | _____ |
| 7. | Chairing a meeting | _____ |
| 8. | Making proposals | _____ |
| 9. | Giving criticism | _____ |
| 10. | Providing information to others | _____ |
| 11. | Contributing ideas to a meeting | _____ |
| 12. | Avoiding interrupting | _____ |
| 13. | Making clear what you want others to do | _____ |
| 14. | Giving recognition and praise to others | _____ |
| 15. | Providing positive feedback to others | _____ |
| 16. | Listening at the right time | _____ |
| 17. | Knowing how to change the conversation | _____ |
| 18. | Having the right word for the right occasion | _____ |
| 19. | Knowing how to use the time available to cover the topics | _____ |
| 20. | Your overall conversational control | _____ |
| | TOTAL SCORE | _____ |

## Scoring

*Your score*          *Action required*

**0–20** You probably feel a lot of time and effort is required and a reading of this book is a good start.

**21–40** You probably feel considerable time and effort are needed to improve.

**41–60** You probably feel that with more practice you will improve your performance.

**61–80** You probably feel that you manage most conversations reasonably and could improve slightly in certain areas.

**81–100** You feel that you are able to perform well in conversations and have a high degree of control. This book will reinforce your skills and show you why you succeed.

We shall look at how and when to improve conversation control skills in the following ways:

- when to speak and when to listen

- how to move a conversation from the past to the present and to the future

- why conversational linking is necessary

- how to distinguish between parallel and sequential conversation

- how to raise energy levels in discussions

- how to move between problem-centred conversation and solution-centred conversation

These aspects of conversation control can make a major difference in getting a message across clearly, in motivating people and in solving problems.

# Why Conversation Control is Important to You

In all situations success in conversing effectively is vital to managing people, managing families and contributing socially to your friends. The list of areas where effective conversation control can contribute to your success and quality of your life is comprehensive. Here are a few situations.

- being able to respond to criticism with confidence

- knowing how to get the correct information quickly

- talking to people at meetings in a convincing way

- handling objections and opposition when making a proposal

It is important to manage conversations, otherwise they will manage you. However, not every conversation is difficult. As the figure shows, most of us have our fair share of difficult conversations, but also have a reasonable number of easy meetings.

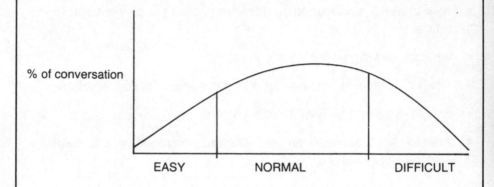

FIGURE 1.1 *How conversations go*

People who are, however, in high stress jobs where they are doing a lot of 'trouble shooting', for example, can expect the most difficult conversations. People in such jobs frequently face situations where they have to consider carefully what they say but do not always have the time to do so. For example, politicians, senior managers, union leaders, some consultants and community leaders are regularly put in the spotlight. There is increasing evidence that such stress situations can create physical illness, such as ulcers and heart attacks, along with other stress symptoms such as sleeplessness and irritability. Therefore being able to control your conversation is a key skill, particularly in difficult circumstances. It gives you time to think and a way in which to respond in a positive and purposeful way.

- finding out where people are coming from and going to

- developing special skills in interviewing and appraisal

- learning to use the dynamics of conversation for both problem-solving and social use with friends.

Therefore your success in life is dependent, to large extent, on your conversational control skills – not only in what you say, but how and when you say it and, most importantly, how you listen and respond.


# Benefits of Conversation Control

You can see the value of skilled conversation control in the results you get from meetings. Others will tell you that they found meeting you a rewarding and helpful experience. You will find you get through your business meetings more quickly. You will be more satisfied with the outcome of meetings. Those who work with or for you will be more highly motivated as a result of the conversations they have with you. Some of the tangible benefits you will see as your command of conversation control increases are the following:

- an ability to get to the heart of matters quickly

- an enhanced ability to understand others

- an improved ability for recognizing cues and clues

- an easier way of responding, particularly when under pressure

- tho fact that you know what you are doing in a conversation.

Because conversation control is central to everything we do, we will see the benefits not only in our work life but in our home with our family and with our friends in social relations.

Managers often tell me that the major problems they face are in responding to the concerns and problems of others and trying to influence people. In particular they emphasize it is important:

7

- to be able to manage conflict

- to negotiate more effectively

- to develop listening skills

- to learn how to be firm without giving offence

- to persuade and influence

- to get people to work together

- to facilitate problem solving

- to get people to think more creatively about the job

- to get others more involved in planning and implementation

The skills outlined in this book provide you with the knowledge necessary to deal with these issues effectively.


# Guidelines

It is no use having a lot to say unless you can say it. Equally, it is no use wanting to find out what goes on if you do not know how to obtain that information from others, by asking questions in the right way and behaving appropriately. We shall be looking at these aspects of conversation control, but beyond this we shall look at specific skills, such as:

- moving conversations from one wave-length to another

- how we can get an in-depth understanding of what others are saying

- ways in which we can get 'on side' rather than 'off side' with others

- techniques for slowing down or speeding up conversations

- methods of improving our conversational problem-solving

Throughout there are numerous examples and illustrations highlighting the need for practice. Conversation is a skill and it can be improved by practice and experience.

# Exercises

An example of how important it is to control conversation occurred when I was visiting a large manufacturing organisation recently. While I was talking with the personnel manager the telephone rang. He took the call, apologizing to me that it must be urgent. I could see that as he listened he was annoyed with what he was hearing. He put the phone down after a while and said: 'It looks as if we are going to have a work stoppage, owing to one of our technical managers saying the wrong thing'.

Apparently a senior technical manager had gone into one of the operational areas and had seen one of the shop-floor workers mixing some chemicals in what the technical manager regarded as a dangerous way. He had immediately gone up to the person concerned and publicly criticized him.

It was later alleged that the technical manager had said 'What the bloody hell are you doing with that mixture? You stupid idiot! Can't you read the instructions? Get your supervisor while I get the safety officer'. This conversation was overheard by other members of the workforce. When the supervisor appeared, he was also verbally abused.

The personnel manager said 'The technical manager may be correct but he has opened his mouth in the wrong way at the wrong time'. The shop-floor worker had complained to the shop steward and a stop-work meeting had been called.

This is one illustration of why conversational control is critical at work. Every day we all have to use conversational skills to communicate our point of view and hear other people's. Studies show that on average managers spend between 75 and 80 per cent of their time talking to others. Conversational control skills are therefore central to effective managerial performance.

(a)   How should the technical manager have behaved when he entered the operations area and saw the dangerous situation?

(b)   As the personnel manager, what will you say to (1) the technical manager and (2) the shop steward?

# CHAPTER TWO

# How to Recognize Cues and Clues

'Men occasionally stumble over the truth but most of them pick themselves up and hurry off as if nothing had happened.'

*Sir Winston Churchill*

---

All conversations and discussions are full of cues and clues as well as signs and signals. They indicate what is important and not important. The person who is skilled in conversation control will quickly identify the key cues and clues and build on them. Others who do not hear or see them will miss the opportunity, and the conversation will probably fail. Therefore we shall look at:

- examples of cues and clues

- how to identify and use them

- how to interpret signs and signals

- their use in conversation control

---

## Disguised Messages are Normal

What are cues and clues? They are the words used to draw attention to what people believe to be important. We can do this not only with our choice of words but the tone of voice used. In every conversation you are indicating to someone else through your cues of key words what you consider to be important; likewise the other person will give some clues on what they feel is important. The conversation will only succeed if you can both build on these cues and clues. Very often people give some of

11

their most important clues through non-verbal behaviour: The shrug, the hand over the mouth, the lean backwards or forwards in the chair, the clenched fist. We shall therefore look at this aspect of conversation control. Let us start with cues and clues.

I am continually surprised that people hear but do not understand the verbal clues they get. In my job I have the opportunity of sitting in on many managerial meetings, and so often they fail or fall apart because people do not 'pick up' the cues and clues.

Verbal cues and clues are being given all the time. A cue is a word or phrase you use when you want to give an indication that something is important to you. A clue is a similar set of words, only the key point is that the words are spoken by someone else.

Let me illustrate with some specific examples of how cues are given but not always received. When they are written down, they may appear obvious, but at the time such comments were not picked up by those listening.

A manager was conducting an appraisal interview with his subordinate who said 'I like working here but I don't find the job stretches me very much as I have now got things well organized'. The boss replied 'But I think productivity in your area could be improved'. The subordinate immediately went on the defensive, explaining why productivity had been restricted owing to illness and absenteeism. The appraisal ended, and the subordinate said to a colleague afterwards 'It was a waste of time. He just talked about what he wanted to pick on and did not listen to what I was concerned about. I told him the job bored me and didn't stretch me any more but he just ignored what I wanted to talk about'.'

In another example drawn from real life a manager talking to a consultant about a problem said 'I introduced these changes which I had taken a long time to plan. We ran into some difficulties which I had not foreseen and I did not get the gains expected'. The manager stopped talking and looked at the consultant. He had made an important point. Although he had not said it, the manager was indicating that he had failed. The phrase 'did not get the gains expected' was a roundabout way of giving a cue.

The consultant missed the cue and said 'How long have you been doing the job now?' The conversation immediately lost momentum.

If the consultant had exercised conversation control, he would have followed up the cues by enquiring about the 'difficulties' of introducing the 'changes' and the 'gains' expected. These were all important words, as the manager was still looking for a way to solve the problem.

## Expect Cues and Clues

We all miss cues and clues because often we are not quick enough to observe and understand. People often tell us things in an oblique way. They indicate that they know or feel something but are unwilling to say more unless we pick up the cue and clue. We should therefore expect to receive clues. We need to listen to the important words people use. They can be unusual words, words which are stressed, or just words that do not seem to relate to the situation as you see it.

A good example occurred recently. I received a telephone call from a business acquaintance, who asked for information on what management courses we had that he could go on. I provided the information and the dates. However, I was surprised and asked why he needed another course, as he had only completed one a few months previously. He said 'Well, quite a few things have changed since then'. Here was a clear clue. I enquired in what way things had changed. He then went on to say that he had been promoted but had come across some major behavioural problems with his staff.

So instead of talking about a 'solution', we met and talked over the real problem. He told me he was having difficulties in getting the co-operation of certain people. By identifying the important cues and clues we were able to get beyond the presenting symptoms and to discuss the practical requirements, which comprised changing the organization's reporting system and moving staff into different roles. His original request for a training course was only a clue.

In business we are given clues each day, but because of time pressure do not always hear them or pay attention. People do not always spell things out. Since they may be unsure of their facts or they are not sure how you will react, they only give a hint of what is on their mind. They leave it up to you to show an interest and invite them to say more.


## The Meanings behind The Words

Cues and clues are key aspects of life, but particularly at work. Here are a few examples which illustrate what lies behind a comment.

- 'I notice Bill was not at work on Friday. He seems to be having a lot of days off recently.' (This person knows that Bill is an alcoholic but is not sure whether he should tell his boss, to whom he offers this clue.)

- 'I don't like the way the exchange rate is affecting our costs. It seems to me that things are getting out of control.' (This person knows he cannot meet his budget now that costs have increased, and fears that he will be blamed.)

- 'The applicant has fulfilled his duties here. His performance has been well received in the areas in which he has concentrated. He likes to pursue matters in depth and can be critical of others who disturb his approach'. (A referee's letter, which hid more than it disclosed, for an applicant who was a loner and did not fit into the team, doing only work which was of benefit to himself.)

Say you were having a meeting with one of your staff about his work and he said 'We have been under a lot of pressure recently'. You might reply 'So has everyone; it just means we have to work more efficiently'. Alternatively, you might sense a clue to more important matters underlying the general statement, and enquire 'What kind of pressure?'

'Well, in addition to the extra work at the office, I've had some family problems, as my wife has been in hospital and I have had to look after the three children.' So that is what he meant by 'pressure'. Maybe it would not have emerged if the manager had not picked up the clue word and asked about it rather than making another statement of what was required. At least once the problem is known, it can be tackled in a planned way.

Cues and clues are difficult to handle because they are not always directly visible. Do not always take what people say first at face value. It requires careful conversation control to encourage people to share and talk about things they are not sure they should talk about. The skills in encouraging people to talk through their concerns and problems must not be used for manipulating people or putting them at a disadvantage.

# How to Identify Cues and Clues

First of all a cue is what you offer someone else if you wish to indicate an area of conversation that is important to you. Clues are what you receive from other people on issues they consider important.

How do you know when you are being offered conversational clues? There are some basic principles which are usually sound indicators.

First of all, listen carefully when people use the words 'I', 'me' or 'my'. At that point they are speaking about the most important person in the world – themselves.

Second, listen carefully if people follow up comments about themselves with strong adjectives such as 'disappointed', 'annoyed', 'worried', 'angry', 'concerned', 'unhappy', or other words such as 'excited', 'keen' or 'enthusiastic'. Such words indicate high energy levels.

Third, listen for words which imply the other person is under pressure to do or achieve something. For example, if someone says 'I can't let that happen next time', 'It was a disaster and I must change my approach', or 'The plan did not work and I feel it's my responsibility', he is giving strong personal clues about action that has to be taken in which there is probably a critical time element.

Fourth, listen when people express doubts and concerns. If these sorts of clues appear and you want to help, listen to the personal issues expressed. Ask people what they are going to do next, whom they will talk to, what they will say, when they will do it and how. In this way you will help a person to talk about a matter, and consider options of action.

People often ask if conventional cues and clues are given at a specific time. You cannot predict when people will offer particular cues and clues. If people are in an environment where they feel safe, and trust you, they will often speak more freely. However, people also offer cues and clues when they are under strain and feel the need to talk about their problems.

Apart from the points mentioned above, listen carefully to the first and last few words people use. Sometimes a particular word may be stressed. But the most important thing is that people often stop talking when they have made an important point, not because they have nothing else to say but to see if you are still interested and listening, or if you are embarrassed. It is at this point that you must exercise conversation control by conveying to the other person that you understand the key issues. If you reflect back to the other person these issues with accuracy and empathy, the person will then probably continue, having confidence in your understanding.

# Signs and Signals

Some of the clearest indicators come from people's non-verbal behaviour. The pointed finger to emphasize a point, the hands over the mouth to guard against the wrong word, or the eyes looking upward for help are signs. Non-verbal signs and signals take different forms, in some places depending on the culture. It is vital if doing international business to learn what the non-verbals are in a particular country, as they often speak louder than words.

An important non-verbal clue is how people sit or stand when talking to you. If they adopt a defensive position with hands folded or their body turned away, then this in itself could be a signal they are not necessarily at ease. If, however, they are sitting forward and getting closer to you, this usually indicates they are willing to tell you important information, providing you give them the permission through appropriate questions or reflections.

People often give their strongest cues and clues through various signs and signals. When a person is annoyed, this is usually shown instinctively in the way he or she looks. The body will give the key signs and signals. When persons are relaxed and at ease they will usually smile more and nod their head.

You can therefore observe, without a word being spoken, the attitude of the person. Indeed if you see a person is uptight and showing physical symptoms of strain such as the furrowed brow or the pointed finger, then a first step in calming them can be to indicate you have received the signs and signals by saying 'I can see that you are annoyed by what has happened'. This will not solve the problem but provides a basis for discussing what has caused the problem. By recognizing the signs and signals you are helping to reduce the tension by making the matter discussable.

Signs and signals take many forms, particularly in the office a person has and the way it is furnished, and in the clothes people wear. These can show us how people see themselves and provide a basis for conversation. Although we are concentrating on conversational cues and clues, these are usually accompanied by signs which can give us clear indications of what the people we are talking to feel to be important.

If you are visually aware, you may find it easier to spot the signs and signals people give than to hear the cues and clues. Usually the words and behaviour go hand in hand. You therefore need to look and listen carefully, but, most important of all, ask open-ended questions so that people can tell you more.

# How We Communicate

|  | I Give | I Receive |
|---|---|---|
| Verbal | 1. CUES | 2. CLUES |
| Visual | 3. SIGNS | 4. SIGNALS |

FIGURE 2.1  *The message matrix*

Figure 2.1 shows a quick way to identify messages that are given either by yourself or someone else. The difficulty is in picking them up and responding quickly in a meaningful way. With practice, however, you can learn to improve in both giving clear cues and signals and recognizing clues and signs. Although it is easiest to refer collectively to cues and clues and signs and signals the figure shows the differences for analytical purposes.

1.  Cues refer to verbal indicators that you give to others.
2.  Clues refer to the verbal indicators that others give to you.
3.  Signs refer to the behavioural indicators, such as smiles, groans or hand movements, that you give to others.
4.  Signals refer to the behavioural indicators others give to you.

# Signs and Signals – What Do They Mean?

In conversation everyone engages in non-verbal communication through the movement of their hands, eyes, head, legs and other body movements. Below are listed a number of important such signs and signals. Based on your own experience, what do you think the person engaging in such behaviour would be communicating?

1.  Eyes raised to the ceiling _____
2.  Sitting back hands behind the head _____
3.  Legs crossed, arms tightly folded _____
4.  Sitting forward, hands open, head nodding occasionally _____
5.  Deep breathing, tongue clicking _____

6. Foot tapping, fist clenched _____
7. Hand over eyes _____
8. Direct eye contact – staring _____
9. Fast speech, hands illustrating _____
10. Hand over nose, furrowed brow _____
11. Finger pointing, loud voice _____
12. Eyes down, low voice _____
13. Smiling, hand on your shouler _____
14. Finger over mouth _____
15. Both hands on hip, tight lipped _____

There are many others which you will recognize each day. They all have a meaning and are meant to convey a message. Which are the three or four major signs that you give?

1.
2.
3.
4.

What are the two major signals that encourage you?

1.
2.

What are the two major signals that discourage you?

1.
2.

# Guidelines

Clues and signals are not always easy to pick up. Listen for the key words, the point of emphasis, the adjectives, the intonation and the body movement. Then invite people to say more in the areas that were initially left unsaid. Such conversation control will improve problem-solving, as people put words to their half-thought-out ideas and concerns.

If you want to find out more you can try the following:

- ask people what they mean by the key word
- enquire how the symptoms they describe affect them personally
- find out what the other person has already done to tackle the problems or opportunities and what results, if any, have occurred
- summarize the key cues and clues and invite the other person to say more
- listen in particular for the references to 'I', 'me' or 'my' and personal concerns
- listen for the use of the unusual word and the way it is said
- listen for the doubts and concerns and enquire about them
- build on the clues offered and give people permission to talk
- reflect on the signals they give in their body language and seek to understand them

Watch the signals people make. Observe their defensive movements and also behaviour that indicates more relaxation and a willingness to talk. If appropriate, describe to the other person how they come across to you by saying 'I feel you are worried about this' or 'You seem more at ease now'. By summarizing what you see, your conversation can make the issue discussable.

# Exercises

Here are some examples of situations where cues and clues are offered in business discussions. Assuming you wanted to build on these cues and clues how would you react?

1.  Underline the key cues and clues in the following example. What would you say in the circumstances?

    You are interviewing someone for a clerical job and he says 'I've been unemployed now for sixty-seven days not including weekends. I keep check of the days. It's like a prison sentence. People tell me I need more patience. It's being patient that's getting to me. I want to do something useful'.

*Your response* _____

_____

_____

2. You are invited to act as a consultant to a new manager who has just been promoted in the organization, who says to you 'Our department has gone nowhere for the past five years. We have lacked leadership. Gradually our numbers have dwindled. Now we are being called upon to respond to a lot of big problems. But we are like a starving man who is keen to act, but too weak to do so'.

   *Your response* _____

   _____

   _____

3. You are a member of a committee and one of the members says 'I'm against putting any more money into that project. It's been a disaster right from the start. We have spent money like a drunken sailor and now the time of reckoning has come. I know it will mean a heavy cost in terms of jobs but we must think about the future for all of us'.

   *Your response* _____

   _____

   _____

# CHAPTER THREE

# When to use Problem-centred and Solution-centred Behaviour

'We are more easily persuaded in general by the reasons we ourselves discover than by those which are given to us by others.'

*Blaise Pascal*

---

A major skill in conversation control is knowing when to concentrate on the problem and when to offer a solution. Too often people fail because they offer solutions before they understand the problem. Knowing how to manage the understanding of problems and the development of solutions is a key conversational skill. This chapter will therefore introduce the following important issues:

- the main features of problem-centred and solution-centred conversation

- when to be problem-centred and when to be solution-centred

- how to use the skills

---

In the rush of modern life too many conversations get short-circuited. We are all under pressure to get our message across, to come to a conclusion and move into action. This means we must know how to get to the heart of a problem and then put forward a relevant and practical solution.

This, after all, is what should be the outcome of successful conversation control. Why is it therefore we have so many meetings when the conversation drifts off the point and we go away frustrated at not reaching a solution? The answer lies in how we manage the problem-centred and solution-centred aspects of our conversation.

Problem-centred conversation means you will focus on asking

questions and trying to diagnose the nature and causes of the problem. In contrast, the solution-centred conversation will focus on proposals and directions for implementing action. The difference in the emphasis between these two approaches can have a considerable impact on the problem-solving process.

Consider the following case example and assess how you would respond. The meeting is between Rod Clark, sales manager, and one of his salesmen, Jim Reid. The background to the meeting is that Jim Reid, who has been with the organization for 14 years and is now aged 38, has not been performing as well as he has done in previous years. For the past 12 months, his sales have fallen by over 10 per cent, whilst his colleagues, on average, have increased theirs by 10 per cent. Rod Clark therefore decides to have a talk to Jim Reid:

**Clark:** Jim, I have noticed over the last 12 months that your sales figures have been lower than previously; is there a specific problem?

**Reid:** I've had a few problems in my area with old customers going out of business and that has made it difficult. My area is a tough district in which to do business. There is a lot of unemployment. I've been covering the same territory for the last 5 years, so it's about time I had a change.

How would you respond in such a situation? Let us consider some options:

**Option A:** 'Well, I could arrange a swap to the eastern area if that would be of interest.'

**Option B;** 'What do you mean by having a change?'

Option A is clearly a proposed solution, while Option B seeks to gather more information about the problem that Reid has identified. In each conversation we have to make choices between going for more information on the problem or putting up solutions.

A weakness of those who do not have conversation control skills is that they offer solutions when they should assess problems, and concentrate on problems when they should be putting forward solutions.

There is often a lot of pressure upon us to give solutions, but if we do so without understanding the problem, there is a great danger we will make the wrong choice. Therefore it is important to know when to be problem-centred and when to be solution-centred, as Norman Maier (1963) illustrated with his pioneering work on interpersonal skills development.

One way of looking at problem-centred and solution-centred approaches is to see that one is 'below the line' and the other 'above the line' (Figure 3.1). We shall refer to these shorthand descriptive terms to illustrate the appropriate and inappropriate use of problem-centred and solution-centred conversation.

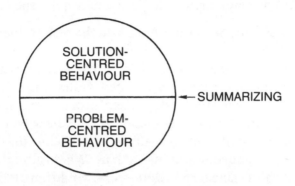

FIGURE 3.1  *Problem-centred and solution-centred behaviour: key aspects of conversation control*

Problem-centred behaviour is concerned with finding out. To do this one must enquire, diagnose and summarize. Those skilled in problem-centred behaviour will find out more from another person more quickly and effectively than those who are unskilled. Of course they will ask questions and get the other person to talk, but it is the manner in which they do it that shows their skill. An example is the way that interviewers on TV, whether it be chat shows or political discussions, encourage others to talk. The good ones make it look natural, the others make us want to turn the TV off.

Solution-centred behaviour is concerned with the giving of proposals, directing and informing. The emphasis is on putting forward ideas, views, methods, systems and options, and solving the problem at hand. Such solutions may or may not work. The way people react to the solution-centred behaviour will be the real test.

Let us therefore return to the case of Reid and Clark and try to recognize the cues and clues that indicate that Jim Reid, the sales representative, does not feel his sales manager, Rod Clark, really understands his problem.

**Clark:** Well, I could arrange a swap to the Eastern area if that would be of interest.

**Reid:** I don't think that would work.

**Clark:** Why not?

**Reid:** Well, it means I would have to travel a long distance or buy a new house.

**Clark:** The company would help you acquire the new home.

**Reid:** Yes, but that would not solve the real problem.

Here is an example where the sales manager quickly becomes solution-centred. But it is inappropriate behaviour as Jim Reid does not see the solution as solving the 'real problem'. Unless Rod Clark is able and willing to pick up the clues being offered by Reid, he will quickly lose control of the conversation. Clearly he needs to 'get below the line' and start asking some open-ended questions such as 'What is the real problem?'

If the sales manager had done so, he would have found out that Reid did have some serious problems at home affecting his work, as well as his own personal concern to gain promotion after so many years as an ordinary sales representative. For example, Reid had a son who needed special education due to an abnormality. This put a lot of strain on the family and Reid had decided reluctantly on a private local-based education for his son to relieve the pressure on his wife. He therefore did not wish to move from his house and neighbourhood, where his family had the support of his in-laws and local facilities. He had not mentioned this problem in any way to his work colleagues, as it was a territory he wished to keep private.

Being problem-centred and encouraging the other person to raise such issues may cause difficulties for some managers when permission is gained to enter territory where such personal problems are revealed. Therefore managers may avoid asking problem-centred questions which are likely to raise such issues. Rod Clark, however, decided to become more problem-centred and found out why Reid was having difficulties. They discussed the problems and decided to reorganize Reid's job and give him some supervisory training should a vacancy occur.

# Problem-centred Skills

There are three main problem-centred skills that can be developed with practice: enquiry, reflection and diagnosis.

## ENQUIRY

Questions are the basis of any enquiry. In order to get the right information you need to move from open questions to closed questions and vice versa on a regular basis. The manner and tone in which one enquires is often as important as the question asked. The main forms of enquiry tend to be closed questions demanding specific responses and open questions requiring an expression of feeling or opinion.

For example, in the meeting, Clark, the sales manager, could get information in the following ways.

'What sort of opportunities are you thinking of?' (open question)
'Is the problem that you are getting bored with the job?' (closed question)

The way we enquire and the questions we use determine our effectiveness in conversation. It is important therefore to distinguish between the various forms of enquiry. There are three major forms of questions. These are:

(a) open questions
(b) closed questions
(c) leading questions

An open question is one that allows the other person to choose the territory on which he/she responds, although by your question you will indicate the area that you wish them to address. For example, the following are all examples of open questions:

'How are things going at work?'
'What sort of a holiday did you have?'
'How are you?'

The questions indicate a general area of interest but do not constrain the other person in his/her response.

The *closed* question is specific. It invariably requires a factual or yes/no kind of answer. The question not only specifies the territory but the particular area of response. The following are examples of closed questions:

'How long have you worked here?'
'What time is it?'

'How far is it to the city from here?'
'Have you finished that job I asked for?'

Closed questions are useful for getting to the point quickly. A doctor usually asks a lot of closed questions to identify particular symptoms, and follows up with other specific questions requiring yes or no answers. Asked in the right way by someone who has your permission to do so, closed questions are vital to efficiency in conversation. However, if you need to form an opinion then you must move to open questions and enquiry.

*Leading* questions can speed conversation up or stop it altogether. A leading question usually implies that the answer is already known and you are only being asked to confirm it. Police interrogators use it to establish that they 'know' the answer when sometimes they may be guessing. The leading question can therefore be useful to speed up confirmation of opinions and facts.

Examples of leading questions are:

'Would you not agree with me that it was unwise to spend that money
without consulting others?'
'How often do you beat your spouse?'

As you can see, the leading question can lead you into argument and contention. As a form of getting information on a problem it should only be used when you are sure of your information and you are seeking confirmation, as most people do not like to be trapped or manipulated in conversation.

## DIAGNOSIS

If you try to identify the cause of the problem, you will be providing a diagnosis. Doctors do this regularly. If you consult the doctor with a stomach pain, he/she might say 'The problem is that you have a pain in the stomach because you have an ulcer'. This gives you a problem-centred response, but the solution has not yet been offered. All conversation that provides a specific cause will be diagnostic and should be used to get at the nature of problems.

In all business conversations you will hear people making diagnoses. For example, people will say things like 'We are not making the sales because we do not follow up our adverts with personal calls' or 'The reason production is down is that we have no room there for buffer stock and there is a delay in getting material from the warehouse to the factory floor'.

Now these diagnoses may or may not be correct. They are opinions that need to be supported by fact. However, where you have opinion and fact, there is a need to see if the interpretation is correct. Take, for example, 'The problem is that we are only renewing 60 per cent of our subscriptions and this means we shall fall 30 per cent below budget, which will cause a negative cash flow of about 100,000.' All this is very specific, but is it accurate? Diagnosis must be accurate and skill in conversation control can help improve the way people find out what is wrong.

## Solution-centred Skills

As Figure 3.2 shows, there are two major ways in which you can be solution centred. These are:

- to propose – this includes suggesting, prescribing, putting up ideas, or recommending

- to direct – this includes telling, instructing and giving firm orders

In any conversation you will use both approaches. They will be closely tied to solution information, where you provide some data before directing or proposing.

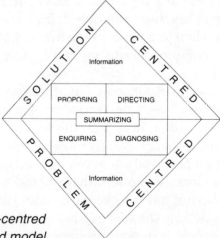

FIGURE 3.2  *Problem-centred and Solution-centred model*

27

## DIRECTING

Here you tell someone exactly what you want done, when and how. In this way you are clearly stating the solution and, more specifically, what the other person has to do.

When should you direct or tell someone what to do? There are some general rules worth using. For example, it is appropriate to direct or tell someone when:

(a) you know what the problem is
(b) you know what the solution is
(c) you believe that solution is acceptable

Where these three conditions exist, make a decision and tell people what you want them to know and do. However, where any one of these conditions is missing, maybe you should become problem-centred.

Very often we know the problem and have a solution but we overlook how acceptable such a decision could be. If we proceed without consultation, then the solution may be rejected regardless of its technical merit. So ask people what they think of your solution if possible before you implement it.

## PROPOSING

Here you are making suggestions and recommendations. You put forward your ideas, but are willing to listen to other people's views. You may therefore change your mind in accord with what people say in response to your proposal.

At times people confuse directing and proposing, particularly when it suits their convenience. If a subordinate makes an error based on your proposal, he/she may say 'But I was only doing what you told (directed) me to do'. Equally when you issue a directive and others do not implement it, they may come back and say 'But I only thought you were making a proposal'.

Proposals are powerful in conversation, since they require a response. People tend to have three ways of responding. They may move closer to your proposal, move further away and withdraw, or attack your proposal. We shall look at these behaviours more closely as we proceed.

You should make a proposal when you have an understanding of the problem and some workable options that you feel will be acceptable to the other person. Do not put your proposal until you see that person is ready. If in doubt, ask if he/she wishes you to outline some ideas. Do not be discouraged if people turn your proposals down. Listen carefully to their objections. This is a key rule in selling, whether it be as a professional activity or just selling your car or home. Only by adapting your proposal to the needs of others, in line with their objections, can you gain success.

Proposals are a vital element on the road to action. Build proposals on an understanding of the problem, on the facts and on the feelings of what others need, and you won't go far wrong.

We all have had a lot of experience at making proposals. It is often a favourite pastime, particularly when it comprises giving advice to a friend, or better still indicating how various political problems should be solved. You can tell a proposal by the introduction it gets. Here are a few examples:

'If I were you, I would . . .'
'Why don't you . . .'
'In my experience the best way to tackle that is . . .'
'I suggest you . . .'
'I think the best idea would be to . . .'
'What they would do if they were sensible would be to . . .'

Most of us are world experts at proposals, even if we do not always have a detailed knowledge of the problem. Indeed, on occasions it can be most helpful just to have a range of options and ideas put forward so you have a range of choices. However, if people say such things as 'that idea wouldn't work' or 'you don't really understand the situation', then get below the line and become problem-centred to find out what the person really means.

Proposing can take the form of bargaining rather than just the exchange of ideas. People who like to trade will often put a proposal as a form of bargain. They offer a quid pro quo, i.e. they will help you solve a problem if in return you will help them. Therefore the proposal is put as a form of exchange: 'I can contribute and help if you will . . .'

# Summarizing

Of all the conversational skills the art of summarizing is one of the most important. It is for this reason that Chapter 10 is devoted to it later in the book. For our purposes here, though, it is important to outline the nature of summarizing and its place in the problem-centred/solution-centred model.

Summarizing is placed exactly in the middle of the circle between the lower half problem-centred section and the top half solution-centred section in Figure 3.1 because it is concerned with both problems and solutions. It is just as important to be able to summarize a problem as it is to summarize a solution.

Summarizing is the way in which you can move between problems and solutions. Indeed as a rule it is valuable not to put forward a solution until you have summarized the problem to the satisfaction of those present. There can of course be exceptions, such as when you are having a creative brainstorm session. Likewise it is important before you move to a decision and action that you summarize the solutions and reasons for the choice that has been made. This will help reduce the possibility of future disagreement.

By summarizing you provide a series of checkpoints during a meeting so people can build on what has gone before. It is valuable to summarize when you want to change topic, secure agreement, or check understanding. Most people could improve their conversational effectiveness a lot by spending more time accurately summarizing, as in that way others could see they were listening and understanding.

## REFLECTION

This is a particular summarizing skill. By picking up the key words people use and reflecting them back you can indicate you are willing to hear more of their problem. Someone might say 'I'm not sure I'm doing the right thing'. If you want to reflect, you would say 'You feel you might be making a mistake'. This picks up the cue words and gives the other person permission to continue talking about the problem if he/she wishes. Skilled reflection is an important part of conversation control.

An example of this would be if Clark in the case study said 'You are concerned that you have been working in the same area for 5 years and want a change'. This reflection of what Reid has said, if done properly, will give him the chance to continue.

It is important to reflect the exact meaning of what the other person says, otherwise he/she will reject your reflection and feel you have not listened. Therefore do not interpret what they say, do not add to what they say and, do not question or criticize what they say. If you wish to reflect, play back the feelings expressed.

To do this in a way that carries conviction your body language must say what your words say. Therefore lean forward in a non-aggressive emphatic way, genuinely interested and concerned. Above all relax and ensure that the other person is aware that you are focusing attention on not only what he/she says but him/her as a person. In this the way you use your eyes is important. While it is vital you maintain eye contact, do not stare or express surprise in the way you look at the person.

Reflecting is a key conversational skill. It acts as a lubricant in conversation. If you reflect well, it enables the other person to continue and add to the points he/she has made. Above all it allows the other person to control the topic, territory and speed of the conversation. It is therefore important to use reflection for the benefit of the other person rather than just yourself. If you do this, they will have the chance not only to communicate their views to you, but also think and clarify points for themselves.

# Guidelines

1. Be problem-centred when you are not sure of the facts or the feelings.

2. Be problem-centred when a closer identification of the problem will help with the formulation of a solution.

3. Be solution-centred when you have the facts and feelings and have sufficient technical competence to make a choice.

4.  Be solution-centred when you feel it is time to put forward a proposal.

5.  When in doubt, keep 'below the line' and be problem-centred.

6.  Regularly summarize before you change topic or reach a decision.

To be solution-centred means that you are putting up ideas, views, directions, propositions and/or suggestions of how a problem could be tackled. In the Clark/Reid case, Rod Clark could have been directive by letting Reid know he could not change his area. Alternatively the manager could have been solution-centred in a different way by proposing an idea for improvement, such as going on a sales course or offer some form of negotiation to add an incentive for improvement. These solutions of course would not have dealt with Jim Reid's problems. His boss might therefore have felt Reid was just a difficult person who was unwilling to move despite the well intentioned solutions.

We need to be skilled in both problem-centred conversation and solution-centred conversation. Table 3.1 shows some of the initial approaches used by people when they are being problem-centred or solution-centred.

As a general rule it is more appropriate when in difficulties to 'get below the line' and become problem-centred to find out more. Then you will have a stronger base upon which to become solution-centred. The practice of problem-centred and solution-centred behaviour is a key to conversation control.

TABLE 3.1

| Problem-centred | Solution-centred |
| --- | --- |
| I ask | I suggest |
| I reflect | I offer |
| I listen | I recommend |
| I inquire | I advise |
| I inform | I inform |
| I research | I propose |
| I search | I direct |
| I diagnose | I tell |
| I gather | I develop |

# Exercises

1.  How would you rate these questions in terms of the problem-centred or solution-centred emphasis?

    **A.** I suggest it would be a good idea to replace the lock on that machine.

    **B.** What in your view are the causes of the machine break down?

    **C.** Wouldn't it be a good idea if you moved to the day shift?

    **D.** When did the system start to fail?

It is clear that A and C are solution-centred questions. Items B and D are problem-centred. Item B asks an open-ended diagnostic question. Item D concentrates more specifically on the time the problem occurred.

These simple examples show the value of conversation control by using problem-centred and solution-centred skills. We shall build on these as we proceed and show other aspects of problem-solving behaviours.

2.  In your own conversation, how could you improve the following?

(a) Your problem-centred skills

_____

_____

(b) Your solution-centred skills

_____

_____

3.  If people made the following comments to you, what would you say to reflect their concern, assuming you were their superior?

(a) I have had two meetings with the project group to try and get them to work together more effectively, but I don't seem able to get through to them.

_____

_____

(b) There are parts of the job I don't like and therefore I give them a low priority. I dislike, for example, the paperwork and I have now got myself in a mess with various documents missing. I think I should probably move to another kind of job.

_____

_____

(c) I have just been to the doctor who says I am suffering from high blood pressure and should take things easy for a while. I've had a difficult time at home recently and this has made it difficult for me to concentrate at work.

_____

_____

# CHAPTER FOUR

# How to Change Conversations Through Statements and Requests

'You made some good statements when you started asking questions.'

*Anon*

---

Every time you enter a conversation you will be making either a statement or a request. These two aspects are therefore central to conversational control. You need to know when to use statements and when to use requests and how to move from one to another. We shall consider:

- when to make requests and when to make statements

- how to gather specific and general information

- what conversational linking is and its use

---

Many discussions turn into arguments because people do not know how to control their conversation. Those who are skilled in managing conversations know how to give and gain information and will more frequently have successful problem-solving meetings than the unskilled.

Statements and requests are the building blocks from which successful problem-solving of major problems can develop. All conversations need the right balance of statements and requests. Too often people make statements when they should make requests.

One of the major criticisms I hear as I visit organizations is that senior management does not listen. I also hear from senior managers that upward communication from staff in the organization is poor. Can they both be right? I therefore look at the way people converse and in particular how they make statements and requests. I have found that where staff feel that managers don't listen they say that such managers are making a lot of statements, but few requests. In short they see the conversation as rather one-sided. Equally, I have met senior managers who tell me that their staff make a lot of requests but give few statements on how they see the problems being resolved.

Look at your own relationships and see who are the recipients of your statements and requests. Because we make statements and requests every day, it does not seem a difficult part of managing conversation. We are all used to making statements, some of which have the desired effect and some which do not. Either requests or statements can be seen as attacks which involve a 'put-down' or an acceptable contribution with 'no put-down'. This can be seen in the matrix in Figure 4.1.

|  | No 'put-down' | Put-down |
|---|---|---|
| Request | + | – |
| Statement | + | – |

FIGURE 4.1  *How people react to your communication*

Every time you make a request or statement it will be seen as a plus or minus by the person you are talking to, and they will react accordingly, depending on whether it is a helpful, supportive contribution or a 'put-down'. You can see quickly how people react by the look on their face. If it is a put-down, they will usually scowl and try to interrupt you. If it is not a put-down, they may smile or nod and offer you some helpful information.

Given this way of looking at conversations, how do you assess the following:

- 'I will be going out at 10.00 am to a meeting and be back by 11.00 am.'

- 'I will have to get my driver's licence renewed.'

- 'I am fed up with the way you waste time.'

- 'If I've told you once, I've told you a thousand times not to put the materials in that drawer?'

- 'You did that on purpose.'
  'I did not.'
  'Oh yes, you did.'
  'Oh no, I didn't.'

These are all statements but they can clearly have very different results. The reason is that some are personal statements which may only affect yourself while some statements affect others in a positive or negative way.

Even a statement like 'I will be going out at 10.00 am . . .' can bring resistance and a counter statement if it cuts across another person's territory and level of permission. They may reply 'You can't do that, as you agreed with me to resolve the new product plan which I have to deliver later today'.

However, when you put someone else down with a statement such as 'I am fed up with the way you waste time', be prepared for a counter statement. Very rarely do people come back with a request in such circumstances. They will normally reply with a denial, such as 'I'm not wasting time', rather than 'Can you tell me specifically what you mean by wasting time?'

When you get into this exchange of accusatory statement followed by denial, you are locked into the 'yes, you did; no I didn't' game as shown in the last example above. This is a favourite of young children but is played equally well by adults.

Making a request can also be done in various ways. Again you can test your initial reaction to the following:

- 'Can you tell me what time the next train arrives?'

- 'Why don't you turn it upside down, as that will help it work better?'

- 'Why do I have to do everything for you?'

- 'How to you feel about that?'

These are just four of the many forms of request you can make. The first is a straightforward request for facts. There is no put-down. The second is a solution suggestion framed as a rhetorical request. The third is also a rhetorical request framed more as a put-down of the other person. The fourth is an open-ended request for a person's feelings on a specific issue. The reaction to each request depends on how the other sees the request, based on the relationship he or she has with you.

Requests can therefore bring a defensive or positive response, depending on the tone with which you make it and whether or not you are infringing someone's personal territory. If you do, then they will usually respond to deny you further access and probably seek to attack your territory.

Therefore making appropriate statements and requests are crucial to problem-solving. If your conversation is not going well, examine your contribution. Are you making too many statements and not enough requests, or, on the contrary, making too many requests when the other people want to hear you make some useful and relevant statements?

Let us look at one example to show how a manager successfully managed a conversation to get a result from a situation where statements by themselves were not working.

## Case Example – Why Does the Conversation Fail?

Russ McDonald is the sales manager and John Gale the production manager in a company that makes boxes for agricultural produce. Russ met John Gale in his office late one Monday evening and the following conversation took place:

**Russ McDonald:** We've just got a big order from Topco. They said they must have it delivered by next Friday otherwise they will go elsewhere.

**John Gale:** We are not geared up to take a big order by next Friday. All the machines have been set up and it will take a lot of time to reset them.

**Russ McDonald:** Yes, but I have been chasing Topco for a long time. This is the first big order they have given us.

**John Gale:** That may be so but you should find out if we can do the job before you go off making wild promises. There's no way we can do a big order by Friday. We are fully stretched.

**Russ McDonald:** You production people get me down. It takes me ages to get an order from Topco and then you are not prepared to put yourself out to supply them.

It is clear that this conversation is on a collision course. Neither McDonald nor Gale seem interested in exercising conversation control. Both are intent on getting across their point and blaming the other person. Such behaviour is not going to resolve the problems which are that:

1. McDonald has made a promise to Topco about the supply of materials by next Friday.

2. Gale has said that he cannot supply the product by that time.

In conversational control terms this meeting is failing because both people, despite the rights and the wrongs of the issue, are not controlling the conversation. We can look at what is happening in terms of the way they manage their requests and statements. Where do you consider the conversation is taking place when examined in the context of Figure 4.2?

|  | General information | Specific information |
|---|---|---|
| Requests | 1. Open questions | 2. Closed questions |
| Statements | 3. General statements | 4. Detailed statements |

FIGURE 4.2  *Giving and gaining information model*

39

Clearly both McDonald and Gale are making one statement after another, and the statements tend to be more general than specific. In all conversations it is difficult to get to the centre of a problem unless people start making some specific requests for information rather than just reiterating statements and blaming others.

As McDonald and Gale were having this conversation, Don Harper, their manager, was passing by and enquired what the problem was. He knew that McDonald was a bit impetuous at times and that Gale could be a bit conservative and pessimistic. Rather than blame either party he decided to exercise some conversation control that he had learned on one of our workshops. In particular he decided to focus his conversation initially on:

- requests

- specific information

- factual information

**Harper:** How big is the Topco order?

**McDonald:** They want 50,000 boxes 10 × 8 size.

**Harper:** When do they want it?

**McDonald:** They said by next Friday.

**Harper:** What time?

**McDonald:** I suppose mid-day

**Harper:** John, how long will it take to set up 10 × 8 to run 50,000?

**Gale:** Some of the machines are already doing 10 × 8 now.

**Harper:** Are those orders urgent or for stock?

**Gale:** I think some are urgent but we are also making some for stock.

**Harper:** Look, we need to see how we can resolve this issue. Russ, you get back on to Topco and ask them when do they need the delivery. Is it early Friday or will Monday morning do as they probably won't use them over the weekend? John, you have a look at the priorities and the making for stock position. Also check what it will cost to run a weekend shift if necessary.

Here Don Harper is clearly exercising conversation control and acting as a link person. He changes the conversation by making a lot of specific requests for facts. Before that the conversation had been exactly the opposite, with both parties concentrating on general statements about personal feelings.

Now this is a simple but effective example of conversational control. The result of this intervention was that McDonald found out that Topco did not need the boxes till Monday morning and Gale came back to say that with the boxes being made for stock plus some weekend work the job could be done. Harper had changed what could be a major conflict into a problem-solving meeting.

# How to Use Conversational Linking Skills

This is a most important skill in conversation. Quite simply it means the ability to move the conversation from point A to point B by a linking mechanism. Therefore, rather than abruptly changing direction, you can steer the conversation.

In essence Harper acted as a managerial link between Gale and McDonald. He produced a problem-solving discussion out of a conflict. He moved the conversation from the past to the present and to the future by a series of linked questions.

Conversational linking can be done in various ways. Here are some examples you can use to move a conversation on by linking what has happened to what should happen.

'Given what you were saying before about our schedules, how does your present proposal fit in?' (Here is a clear link between what has gone and some new information.)

'To what extent do you think the adaptation of the existing building is feasible, given the new machinery we have on order?' (Here again the link is between a concern for the space available in the context of a decision already made.)

'Given what the previous speaker has said, then I believe we should bring together the various parties to hear their views.' (Here the link has been made to widen the debate but basing it on previous contributions.)

Those who are skilled in conversation control are invariably good at conversational linking. They do this by:

41

- relating the past to the future

- relating the problems to solutions

- relating the requests to the statements

- moving the conversation forward from the negative to the positive

## Problem-centred and Solution-centred Revisited

All conversations will depend for their success on how you handle the discussion of problems and solutions. In the case outlined above both McDonald and Gale had solutions. As far as McDonald was concerned, he had made a big sale and that was a solution which everyone should be pleased about. As far as Gale was concerned, he had a solution based on a production plan that he did not wish to have disturbed.

So long as both held to their own solution and tried to tell the other what to do, little progress could be made. The way Harper began to exercise some conversational control was initially to become problem-centred. He started by asking a series of questions relating to where the problem really lay. His linking of the conversation was not random or accidental. It followed a logical model which we can use in everyday life, as shown in Figure 4.3.

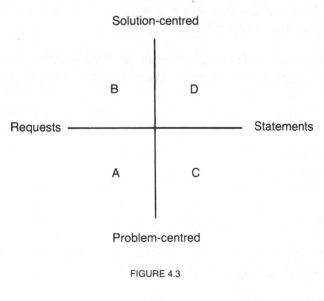

FIGURE 4.3

Harper concentrated initially on Quadrant A in Figure 4.3, where he used problem-centred requests, and worked towards Quadrant B. Then he asked them to come up with some information, and he would probably have expected McDonald and Gale to return to the next meeting with information primarily in Quadrants C and D. This information would then be the basis for further requests and statements. In this way he managed the conversation to get results and used his conversational linking skills to succeed.

Effective managers are continually doing two things: listening to what a person says and also identifying how best to respond to keep the conversation on the appropriate wavelength. They do not let conversations fail for the want of trying. They seek to solve problems and use conversation control skills to keep people motivated while overcoming the obstacles.

# Guidelines

Requests and statements are the basic building blocks of all conversation. The examples in this chapter show some key aspects of the importance of moving from requests to statements and also from statements to requests.

Clearly you will make statements when you want to give facts or opinions to others. Equally you will use requests when you want to obtain information or gain a reaction to a proposal.

Such conversational control needs to be linked particularly to whether you are being solution-centred or problem-centred. In any conversation you need to know when to move from below the line to above the line and vice versa, and to the left or right of the line, as shown in Figure 4.3. Note that:

1. Requests can be made to gain facts, feelings or opinions.

2. Requests can be open-ended, inviting people to say what they want, or closed, to give a specific response.

3. Requests can be solution-centred as well as problem-centred: for example, when you ask people what they think about one of your ideas.

4. Requests should also be used when you want time to think.

5.  Statements can communicate facts, feelings or opinions which are either problem-centred or solution-centred.

6.  Statements enable you to lead the conversation and control the territory for discussion.

7.  Statements should be used when you want to assert your position or propose a line of action.

Above all, think of yourself as a conversational linker. Practise the skills of building on the key points and moving the conversation forward.

# Exercises

1.  Read the dialogue on the Topco case and assess what Russ McDonald and John Gale could have done to resolve the problem if Don Harper had not intervened.

2.  At your next managerial meeting keep a record of the contributions for a period of time – say 15 minutes – and see where the contributions have got.

3.  Assess your own conversation. Where do you think most of your contributions are? Where you have a low number of contributions, try to practise in the areas of the models.

# CHAPTER FIVE

# How to use Time Dynamics in Conversation

'Those who make the worst use of their time are the first to complain of its brevity.'

*La Bruyere, 1688*

---

All conversations are situated in some period of time. They relate to what has happened, what is happening, or what could happen. The problem is that everyone in a conversation does not always use the same time dimension. Therefore difficulties occur when some people are talking in the past, some in the present and others in the future. We need therefore to cover:

- the time dimensions of conversation

- identifying causes and consequences

- using the past, present and future levels of conversation to advantage

- how to move a conversation forwards or backwards

---

You can improve your conversation control by a better use of time dynamics. The first aspect of this is to be able to know how to move conversations between the past, the present and the future. The second aspect is to know how much time to allocate to each and such related parts as problem-centred and solution-centred contributions.

A number of difficulties arise in managing the time dimension in conversation. Let us start by looking at one typical conversation and show how the time dimension affects the information exchange. Peter Brook is the computer manager of a company. His boss, Tony Alsop, who is the general manager, has little knowledge of computers. Try to identify who is controlling the conversation by the use of time dynamics.

45

**Alsop:** I received this note from you with regard to the need for a new computer. Before I put it on the agenda for the next Board meeting, you'd better tell me about this because, as you know, I'm no expert in these matters.

**Brook:** As I see it, we will need to move to a 5180 series computer within the next 2 years. The evidence suggests that business will continue to expand at the current rate of about 15 per cent per annum. We will therefore have outgrown our existing system in 2 years and need to have made the changeover by that time if we are to maintain our present level of service.

**Alsop:** Well that will mean that we have to not only change computer but change supplier.

**Brook:** Yes, the 5180 system is far superior to anything else on the market. It will do the job faster and also have a far wider range of capability in terms of memory.

**Alsop:** But that will also mean considerable extra cost.

**Brook:** Yes, there is no doubt that the total cost of the changeover will be a major capital expenditure item. So far I have identified that we are talking in the range of $15 million for the hardware and, as you know, in due course, say over a 5-year period, the production of software could cost a great deal.

# How to Avoid Losing Control

Let us break into this conversation for one moment to see what is happening. The general manager is in danger of losing conversational control to a computer manager who has already identified what he wants. So far the conversation has been entirely directed to the future, with little concern for what is happening now or what has happened in the past.

While the general manager is concerned to get the best solution, he is also equally concerned that he must not fall into the trap of discussing solutions before the problem has been identified. In addition to recognizing the solution-centred approach adopted by Brook, the manager also needs to see the time emphasis that is being used.

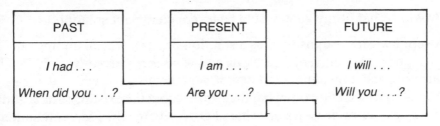

| PAST | PRESENT | FUTURE |
|------|---------|--------|
| *I had . . .* | *I am . . . .* | *I will . . .* |
| *When did you . . .?* | *Are you . . .?* | *Will you . . ..?* |

FIGURE 5.1   *Time dimensions in conversation*

For the moment, Brook, the computer manager, is highly solution-centred and therefore very much orientated towards holding a conversation about future needs. The general manager, in order to exercise conversational control, must start gathering information not only on future requirements but the current and past situation. See Figure 5.1

To do this, he must also seek to identify how far Brook is reflecting not only his own views but those of others. The danger is that he not only gets a future-orientated solution view but also a one-sided single opinion view. Therefore the general manager, Alsop, decides to change the conversation, although Brook is still trying to concentrate on the future:

**Alsop:** What is wrong with the existing system?

**Brook:** Unfortunately it's already outlived its usefulness. It's too slow, it's too costly in terms of breakdown and it's also been superseded by our competitors, who will have the new systems. We must therefore go for the 5180 as quickly as possible.

**Alsop:** To what extent have you discussed your views on the 5180 with the operating managers?

**Brook:** I have not done so yet, apart from informal discussions, as I felt it was important that you and I reach some agreement as to the direction we should go.

**Alsop:** I think it would be useful to take one step back from that and find out what people are actually doing in the departments that require a computer facility. At the moment we have a centralized system. Do people still feel that we should have a centralized system or move towards smaller computers that are adapted to the needs of particular areas?

**Brook:**   That in my view would be a very inefficient solution.

**Alsop:** I wasn't proposing it as a solution but as a way of finding out what people are currently thinking and what they currently need. I will therefore call a meeting of all departmental managers, which you can attend, so we can find out what they think about the existing system and also to gather their views on what changes, if any, they see as required over the next 2 years.

## WHAT HAS HAPPENED?

Within the context of our conversation control model the general manager realizes the discussion is moving too quickly into solution statements and decides that a meeting to focus on the problems would be more appropriate. By having a clear model in his mind of the dynamics of conversation he can assess quickly what is happening. He notes:

- the conversation is moving too quickly into a solution-centred format

- there are too many statements and not enough requests

- the emphasis is too much on the future and not enough on the past and present

His approach is to adopt a medium-term tactic – that of calling a meeting of departmental heads – in order to get to a problem-centred discussion.

In this way the general manager begins to exercise control over a conversation that clearly started at the wrong place. In order to discuss solutions one needs to have some understanding of what the problems are. The general manager was confronted with a computer manager who believed he had a technical solution and had not taken the time to consider people's present comments and views. The general manager sensed this and was able to steer the discussion away from the facts of what the cost would be of installing a new system towards what people's feeling were on the present system.

# Past, Present and Future

Similar problems occur every day in the workplace. Conversations get out of control because people do not manage the time dimension well.

Another example is when the conversation starts in the past and never reaches the future. It often happens when people have a grievance or a grudge to complain about. They get so bound up with airing their grievances that they do not start thinking positively about solutions.

Here is another conversation, this time between a manager and a subordinate. The manager is trying to get the subordinate to think positively about improving his future performance. In contrast, the subordinate is intent upon keeping the discussion in the past.

**Manager:** I have been concerned about your performance over the last few months and feel that I should discuss with you what needs to be done to try to improve this.

**Subordinate:** What sort of things do you mean?

**Manager:** Well, in particular, the reports that you write have been coming in late and have not been up to the usual quality in terms of detail required. Other departments have also indicated that they don't get the information they need on time.

**Subordinate:** Well, there's been a lot of pressure over the last few months. We had more work to do in our section than ever before and in addition I have been trying to complete my part-time course in accountancy.

**Manager:** Well, it's important to reassess your priorities. From now on we need those reports completed fully and on time.

**Subordinate:** I consider my reports have been as good as anyone else's over the last few months. I've certainly worked as hard as everyone else in the team.

**Manager:** Well, in a number of meetings that you have attended, people have raised questions about the figures and we have all sat around waiting for explanations. My view is that the data should have been there at the time.

**Subordinate:** That was the fault of the people who asked me to produce the report in the first instance. They did not ask for that information until the meeting.

## HOW TO ANALYSE THE CONVERSATION

Let us break into this conversation. Already the emphasis is on the past as the subordinate defends his poor performance. He is certainly not allowing the manager to talk to him about the future until such time as the criticism of his poor performance in the past has been resolved. The conversation is therefore locked into the past. The subordinate defends his past activity. The manager wants to move to the future but finds he is blocked. Let us see what is happening by analysing this conversation.

The manager starts with a general reference to the past in his first two contributions, then moves quickly to the future requirements he wants in his third. The subordinate throughout keeps to the past and defends his position. The manager therefore in his last contribution returns to discussing the past, but clearly wants to get to the future.

This is a good example of how conversations can deteriorate. We break into this conversation 15 minutes later and still the manager is trying to move towards the future while the subordinate is talking about the past.

**Manager:** Well, over the next 3 months we want to see some specific improvements in the reports. I think it would be useful if you had a look at some of the documents that are produced by some of your colleagues to give you an idea of the standard that is expected.

**Subordinate:** It seems to me that people are unfairly picking on me. I get the feeling some people are out to get me. As I see it, my work is no worse than anyone else's.

## HOW TO MOVE THE CONVERSATION FORWARD

Clearly the manager is having some difficulty in getting through to the subordinate, and needs to exercise conversation control, by understanding the feelings of the subordinate, even if they are not valid. In short, the manager may have to deal with the past before he can move into the present and the future. To do this he may have to start asking some questions, or perhaps summarizing the understanding he has of the other person's point of view.

**Manager:** I can understand that you may feel that other people are picking on you, given that they consider you have not give them all the information they need. To what extent are you prepared to look at the reports that you write and talk to the people about how you can meet their requirements?

**Subordinate:** Well, providing they are prepared to give me a fair chance like everyone else, I will do my best.

**Manager:** Well, I would suggest that you start by having a look at this particular report which was written on the cost of our water processing plant to see the key points that have come up in that report compared with the one that you did on material handling. As you will see, there is a lot of extra information included. I would like you to use this as a model for the next report that you do. Before you present it to the committee you can discuss it with me if you wish.

In this case the manager:

1.  Lets the subordinate know that he understands how he feels.

2.  Then asks to what extent the subordinate will be prepared to meet the needs of the clients and thereby directs the conversation towards the future.

3.  Then reinforces the future orientation, whilst the subordinate agrees in principle, by giving a specific example of what is required.

In this way the conversation moves from that of one person talking about the past and another person talking about the future to both people talking about the same thing at the same time.

Although here we are focusing on the time dynamics of conversation, the way the discussion moves between statements and requests and problems and solutions is clear.

# Causes and Consequences

Managing is about getting things done. In tackling problems and opportunities you will have to give attention to both the causes of problems and the consequences of taking action. Too often managerial conversations fail because of concentration on causes at the expense of consequences or vice versa.

We have all sat in meetings where we have analysed the cause of a problem inside and out but seem no nearer coming up with a meaningful consequence in terms of action to be achieved. It is the familiar analysis paralysis that comes with an over-concern for cause well beyond what is necessary to identify a basis for action. Equally I have sat in long meetings where a group has agonized over the consequences of a decision without looking too closely at what caused the problem in the first place. Table 5.1 shows the correct procedure.

TABLE 5.1

| Causes | Consequences |
| --- | --- |
| Emphasize the past | Emphasize the future |
| Concerned with 'why' | Concerned with 'how' |
| Attention to reasons | Attention to action |
| Problem-based | Opportunity based |
| Mainly knowable | Mainly unknown |
| Emphasis on facts | Emphasis on possibilities |

Those who are opportunity-minded may forget or ignore the facts. They get 'starry-eyed' about the consequences, seeing what they want to happen rather than what is likely to happen. They then go beyond the evidence and often get into trouble. I was a member of one such group, which had to decide if we should buy a computer book company. At the time we produced journals, and it seemed a logical development. If we could sell journals, surely we could sell books. The whole conversation was on the consequences of buying. We would have better integration, a wider product base, more assets; and so we took such a rosy view of the consequences we did not sufficiently study the other company's reasons for selling.

The result was a near disaster. We did not find out till later that the other company had large outstanding debts which we inherited. Equally we did not discuss the ways in which we could integrate the two businesses. Our conversation had focused too heavily on the consequential benefits we saw and ignored the problems and causes associated with the sale of the computer book company. It was easy to see in hindsight, but it did not seem obvious at the time. We had spent so much time talking about the future that we ignored the evidence of the past and present.

# Guidelines

A skilled person will recognize when a conversation is going out of control because the time dynamics are wrong. When one person is talking about the past and another person talking about the future, it is unlikely that a successful conversation will emerge.

It is usually necessary to deal with the concerns of the past before one can move to the future. In doing that, it is usually equally important to deal with the feelings rather than the facts expressed. This often needs to be done through recognizing, understanding and appreciating the other person's feelings, even if you do not agree with them.

Once this has been overcome, it is then possible to move from the present to the future action, as required, and get commitment from the individuals concerned. Some general principles when problem-solving are:

(a) When someone is proposing a future-based option, consider the past to find out who else has tried it.

(b) When the conversation is in the past, indicate that you recognize people's concerns and summarize before moving it to the future.

(c) When the conversation is in the present, ask what the implications are for the future.

In this way you can change the time dimension of the conversation. It is an important skill because it can refocus the energy towards the time period that will produce the most important data. Very often people plunge into the future without considering the past, or become caught in the past when they should be talking about the present or the future. Causes and consequences are integral parts of all conversations. As a rule causes concentrate on the past while consequences will concentrate on the future.

You need to be able to influence the direction of a conversation if you feel it is not on the right wavelength. If, for example, you feel that there is a need to examine causes in more detail, ask for:

- facts

- examples

- an investigation

- an experiment

- a review

If, on the other hand, you feel the conversation should examine consequences more, then ask for a consideration of:

- a benefits analysis
- a feasibility study
- a test project

By calling for such action you can influence the direction of the conversation and the strategies being pursued. The skill is in reading the time dynamics of the conversation and being quick enough to influence the practice of using the concepts in action.

## Exercises

1. Review a major conversation you have had in the last week. Assess how effectively you used the time dynamics.

|  | Used Poorly |  |  |  | Used Well |
|---|---|---|---|---|---|
| Past, present, future | 1 | 2 | 3 | 4 | 5 |
| Problem-centred | 1 | 2 | 3 | 4 | 5 |
| Solution-centred | 1 | 2 | 3 | 4 | 5 |
| Requests, statements | 1 | 2 | 3 | 4 | 5 |
| Causes, consequences | 1 | 2 | 3 | 4 | 5 |

2. How can you best improve your use of time dynamics in your own conversation?

_____

_____

_____

3. Many people have noted the importance of time and timing in most of life's activity. Here are some opinions that have been expressed. To what extent do you agree with them?

(a) Time is a test of trouble
But not a remedy
If such it prove, it prove too
There was no malady

*Emily Dickinson, 1863*

(b) What reason and endeavour cannot bring about, often time will

Thomas Fuller, *Gnomologia, 1732*

(c) Our costliest expenditure is time

*Theophrastus (c370–287BC)*

# CHAPTER SIX

# Why Territory and Permissions are Important

'There is a tide in the affairs of men,
which, taken at the flood, leads onto fortune.'

Shakespeare *Julius Caesar*

---

In every conversation you will give and receive permission to talk about certain issues. At various points you will feel you should neither ask, nor say any more. You may get a 'red light' refusal. At other times you will get a 'green light' to proceed. Identifying permissions is therefore critical to your success. To do this we shall show:

- how permission is a key conversation control tool

- the importance of conversational territory

- the need to work on the right wavelength

---

## How to Manage Permissions and Territories

It is interesting to watch conversation and see how people react to each other. Very often, particularly in business conversation, people actually look for permission to say various things. They do not actually ask for permission but they are unlikely to contribute unless they feel they have the 'ear' and 'eye' of the other person. Some people of course speak their mind regardless, but in the main most people will only contribute if they feel that they have received permission to do so.

You therefore have to be conscious of giving permission to people if you wish them to speak. We have all been confronted with someone who is about to leave the room and before doing so says 'Do you think the costs on the development project are OK?'

If you are busy you may say 'yes' and that could be the end of the conversation. However, the question really is a cue and a clue that the other person is probably prepared to say more if he/she is given permission to do so.

If you were to ask 'Why, do you think we should look into it more?', you might find some interesting information. In one case this happened and the person who was about to leave turned back and said 'Well I think it would be useful because I was up at the site 2 days ago and one of the people there said to me that there had been a few unforeseen problems and that the breakdowns were leading to a lot of maintenance work and replacement of materials. I also heard a rumour that there had been quite a bit of increase on the cost side due to a mistake that one of the supervisors made by over-ordering some materials'.

Here the junior manager is passing on hearsay and indicating that perhaps the senior manager should look into the issue again. However, if the senior manager had dismissed the first question, then it is possible that the whole matter would not have been brought out into the open. As it happened, the junior manager wanted to spend some time looking into it but needed the permission of the boss to do so. As a result of this discussion, he was asked to make a report and discovered some major cost problems on the project.

# Critical Permissions

People's lives can depend on whether people have permission to say what they really think. Air Florida Flight 90 was taking off from Washington International Airport on 13 January 1982. Outside the temperature was well below zero. As the plane taxied to its take-off position, the first officer began to express some doubts about the flying conditions. These are excerpts of what he actually said (McPherson, 1984):

'This one's (wing) got about a quarter to half an inch (of ice) on it.'

Then later:

'Boy this is a losing battle here on trying to de-ice those things (wings).'

'As good and crisp as the air is and no heavier than we are I'd . . .'

The captain interrupted and the first officer never completed his sentence. Later, however, he said 'Hate to blast out of here with carburettor ice all over me, specially with the (Washington) Monument staring you in the face'.

It was almost as if he knew that a disaster was imminent. He had given cues and clues to the captain but the captain did not give any specific permissions for him to go further. He did not ask his opinion or reflect openly on what the first officer was saying. They therefore continued and disaster struck.

The aircraft did have too much ice on the wings and stalled on take-off. It hit the Fourteenth Street Bridge and fell into the Potomac River. Of the eighty-two people on board only five survived and four innocent people crossing the bridge were killed.

Did the first officer have permission to say what he felt and would it have saved all those lives? We shall never know, but the importance of giving such permission to speak is clearly shown.

# How People Ask for Permission

Some people make it clear that they want permission to discuss certain matters by being direct and to the point. For example, a person who says to you 'I want to spend some time with you to work out a plan for next year' is clearly seeking permission to open up a particular area of conversation. If you agree, this will lead to a discussion of territory in terms of whose area you will discuss, and who will be expected to carry out the plans.

The giving of permission to discuss matters therefore is critical in conversation control. Very often we only get the very faintest clue and we have to be sensitive to pick it up and ask the right question. I sat in a meeting which was discussing how to improve the company's performance by developing new products. One of the managers mentioned that he thought it would be a good idea to start a product in an area previously not tackled by the organization, but the suggestion was not picked up and discussed in detail.

Six months later an organization in direct competition launched exactly the product which the manager had been alluding to. At the following management meeting when the entry of the competitor's product into the market was being discussed, this manager said 'I mentioned that 6 months ago but no one seemed interested in talking about it'. Clearly he felt that he had not had permission to pursue the matter and the whole issue had been dropped until the competitor had come in and seized the opportunity.

### Speak when you are spoken to

Lee Trevino, the world famous golfer, relates an amusing incident. It highlights the absence of permission to speak. The incident occurred on a golf course in one of the major American championships. One of the other international players was renowned for losing his temper and being hot-headed. He had a caddie who talked a lot and went by the name of Snake. Before the competition began the international golfer, who was in a bad mood, said to Snake 'Look, don't say a damn word to me during the whole round. Even if I ask you something, don't say anything'. During the round the international player hit the ball behind a tree. The only way to the green was to hit over a lake and on to the green. The international player sized up the situation and asked the caddie 'Do you think it's a five iron?'

'No' said Snake.

'What do you mean?' said the international player, 'Give me a five iron. Watch this shot.'

The international player hit a beautiful shot straight from under the tree on to the green and it landed 2 feet from the pin. 'There, I told you it was a five iron' he said. 'What do you mean by telling me it wasn't a five iron. What do you think of that shot?'

The caddie looked bemused. 'Well, what's up?' asked the international player. 'You told me not to say anything' said Snake 'but that wasn't your ball.' Permission in conversations is very important even if it is only to get information on golf.

# What Territory Can You Enter?

By giving permission people indicate what territory they will allow you to tread on. This can be either conversational territory or physical territory. I was in a meeting when one person said 'What about the load this new project will put on the staff?' Another manager immediately said 'That's my problem, don't worry about it. I can sort that out'. This manager was saying to the other person that he did not want him or others discussing matters on that aspect of his territory.

Some people are quite specific in the way they indicate their territorial permissions. I met a friend whom I had not seen for a long time and asked about his family. He said 'I've got a few problems there. I'd prefer not to discuss it at the moment'. This was a clear clue to keep off that area of conversational territory.

Some people, however, want you to keep off territory which you feel you have the need and the right to work on. You may, for example, ask for some financial information and the other person says 'I can't provide you with that data because you are not a member of the committee'. Here is a clear case where you are being refused permission. It is here you may need to exercise your assertive skills to gather the information if it is important for you do do your job.

Permission can also extend to physical territory. Consultants, for example, can often be stopped or helped, depending on how they manage their conversation with a client. One person said to a senior manager 'I would like to talk with your staff on the shop floor to gather their views on the problem'. The senior manager immediately replied 'I don't think that would be useful at this stage. There are other people at different levels who would feel we were short-circuiting them'. Here again is a strong cue and clue about territory and you do not have permission to proceed. If you push the point at this stage, you will find resistance becoming stronger until you get a direct refusal.

# Ways to Widen Territorial Permissions

Equally you can get permission to cross organizational territory if you go about the conversation in an appropriate way. In the above example it would have been better to enquire 'Who are the key people we should be talking with about the problem at this stage?' The senior manager would say 'Well, there are various people, particularly the area managers and the union representatives'. You may reply 'To what extent is it feasible to get these people together?' The manager might say 'I could arrange for them to talk to you separately but not both at the same time'. Again the territorial permission is clear.

Permissions are tied very closely to cues and clues. Someone may give you a clue by saying 'We have some problems with motivation'. If you follow this up, you will probably find it is more specific than that and they are willing to give permission to talk about the matter in more detail.

By exercising conversation control you can gain permission to enter territories that would be barred to others. This is clearly important in selling, where you usually need to know what a person is really after. A good example is when you are trying to sell your house. As I have moved home quite a few times over the last decade, I have realized the importance of conversational control in such situations, particularly with regard to permissions and territories. People will often come to look at our house as if they were on a tourist holiday seeing one sight after another. I realized that in order to meet the needs of potential buyers I had to gather information on them and their family. This clearly meant gaining permission to talk on personal territory about their needs, rather than just showing them the house.

In business situations the concepts of permission and territory are central to any effective relation. Each manager has an area or territory for which he/she is accountable. Often they can be defensive about others offering advice, which they see as criticism. They therefore refuse permission to discuss how their work hinders or helps your work. However, with skilled conversation control it is possible to open up a problem-solving relationship in which you give and receive permission to cross onto each other's territory to support and help.


# How People Respond

You can tell what reactions you are getting by observing people's responses. These can be summarized quickly, in line with the analysis made by Karen Horney when she noticed that people will move in three possible ways:

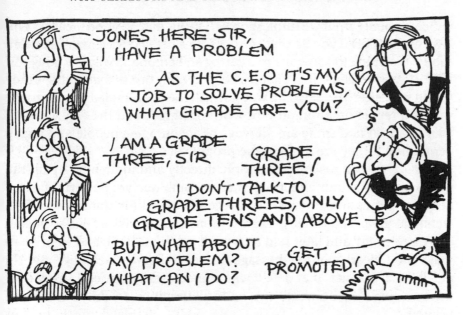

- towards you – problem-solving

- away from you – defensive, withdrawing

- against you – aggressive, attacking

Now these responses depend to a large extent on your own behaviour and how that is received by others. In every conversation you are sending out messages not just with your words but your behaviour, which, as Figure 6.1 shows, will be encouraging, discouraging or ignoring others.

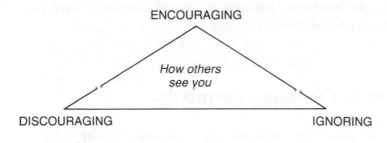

FIGURE 6.1

If we encourage people, we are giving them permission to go in a particular direction. We do this in various ways. Some are to the point and indicate openly what we think such as 'I think that's a good idea' or 'You have my support if you do that'. Other forms of encouragement are more subtle. Listening to someone in a caring and emphatic way is a powerful form of encouragement. It enables people to say things that perhaps they would not otherwise say. The way you ask the open-ended question, the way you reflect on an important word or phrase and the way you nod your head, sit and smile are all ways of encouraging people and giving permission if they are done in the proper way.

Equally we can discourage people directly and indirectly. Again the words and behaviour either together or combined are powerful factors denying permission to proceed. I recently asked for some advice in a technical area. The other person told me that the issues I was raising 'were irrelevant' and later said they were 'not important' and went on in that vein. I clearly got the message he was trying to discourage me. He did it in a manner that I felt was unnecessarily critical. Instead of discouraging me, he made me more determined to find out what I wanted.

Other people discourage you in a perhaps more acceptable way by saying such things as 'If I were you, I wouldn't do that' or 'Given the evidence, I think what you are doing is risky'. Most people don't object to being discouraged if there is some reasonable evidence, it is being presented with their interests in mind, and allows them to make the final decision.

The third form of response is often the most difficult. If people ignore what you say, it can be taken two ways. Either they have no interest in your views and are therefore opposed and will not give permission to enter any territory which they control, or, by ignoring you they may well be saying you have carte blanche and permission to do what you want, providing it does not involve them.

# How to Get People's Permission

People will not always say what they think and feel. They may be shy or concerned that you will deride their opinion. They may just not be sure they can trust you. There are lots of reasons why you do not always find out. However, it can be vital in your job that you do know what other colleagues and team members are thinking, even if it is critical of you and your way of doing things. I was consulting a top manager and he said

'The higher I go in the organization, the less people are prepared to tell me what they really think of how I run things'. We talked for a while and I asked him how he encouraged people to do this. He said it was difficult because most of the meetings were formal. He agreed it would be useful to have a meeting on 'neutral' territory away from the office where his team could talk about how they worked together. I interviewed the team members before the event and found that some members did have strong views which they had never let loose in front of the top manager. When I asked why, they said they were not sure he would listen, particularly as a number of their points were critical.

I indicated to the top manager this general concern without identifying the managers in question. The response from him was 'I might not like what they say about how I run things but if I don't find out then neither myself nor the team can improve'. He therefore organized a weekend workshop at a country club and in so doing indicated that people had permission to talk about his style and the way the team worked. As a result, team members 'for the first time', as one person said, 'really got down to fundamentals on what was helping and hindering their performance'. By showing an example the top manager had given permission for people to open up discussion on important territory. There was a feeling that this 'cleared the air and produced a better working relationship'.

So if you want feedback from others, you have to indicate they have permission to contribute. Often just telling people does not have the right effect. You have to set up the conditions, the time, the place and indicate both by word and deed that people have permission to do things, particularly when you are introducing new and possibly risky ideas or, for example, reviewing someone's performance.

In most organizations now there is some form of performance appraisal, where a manager meets each member of staff to review what they have done, to counsel on improvements and set goals for the future. Most people agree that this is an excellent idea in theory, but very hard to do in practice.

The reason for this is that it necessitates discussing personal matters such as what you have done, or not done and why. Many people are reluctant to open up. Some managers therefore ignore this and insist on moving on to the other person's territory whether they have permission or not. This is usually resisted, particularly if they adopt a judgmental and evaluative approach such as 'I have noticed over the last couple of months your sales have been poor and your attitude to the job is lacking in enthusiasm. If you put more effort in, and take a most disciplined approach, you would be better'. Now this may be true, but the critical diagnosis followed by the quick-fire general solution is likely to lead to a defensive or aggressive response. It is unlikely the subordinate will give many permissions for the manager to really find out what he thinks, so how can the manager get people's permission to be open in sensitive areas?

The first is to give people an opportunity to assess themselves, i.e. the subordinates should be asked to write their own appraisals and these become the basis for discussion. In this way the manager can respond to the subordinates' points, preferably in a supportive and helpful way. If the subordinate does not raise the key issues, then the second rule is to provide some evidence for opening up the conversation in the difficult area and then ask the other person how he/she feels about the situation. If that fails to work then the third rule is to indicate that you are concerned about the situation and ask the other person what he/she will do to improve it. If he/she still refuses to give permission to discuss the matter, you may have to terminate the relationship if all other avenues fail.

# Guidelines

In conversations people are always giving cues and clues that signify what they consider is permissible. Such cues and clues also indicate the territory they will or will not allow you to cover – both physical and mental. If you miss these permissions, the doors may be shut to that territory.

People request permissions in various ways, such as:

- the use of an unusual word in a sentence which puts a stress on the issue under discussion – 'I would say if we don't look at this finance problem now, we could be in *deep water* very soon'

- an identification of an area of doubt or difficulty with a willingness to discuss it – 'I am not sure we should invest without more information. We need *an opportunity* to see how other operators work'

- the references to particular issues and the expression of interest in exploring them further – 'I think the project is an interesting idea and relates to some of *my own thoughts*'

However, not all permissions are clear cut. Listening to the emphasis people give words or reading their body language can indicate what sort of permissions you are receiving. Permissions of course indicate how far you can go in a discussion. You will sense how open other persons are to letting you explore their territory by their tone of voice, their facial expression, their hands and their attitude towards you.

Everyone has territory they wish to protect. However, it is the person with effective conversation control who can often find out the most from others in a quicker time. They are allowed to travel over territory that will be otherwise protected. They are given permission to talk in areas not open to others.

We all protect our conversational territory until we find people who we feel we can trust with private and important information. Therefore the cues and clues people give need to be recognized and treated with respect if we are to be skilled in conversation control.

# Exercises

1. Consider situations where you have refused someone permission to discuss a particular area which you felt should not be brought into a conversation. What were the key issues?

(a) _____

(b) _____

(c) _____

2. In conversation you control territory. If a journalist from a newspaper came to your office to talk about your work, what are the territorial topics you would be prepared to let them know and write about and which would you avoid?

| Open areas | No-go areas |
| --- | --- |
| | |
| | |
| | |

3. Can your remember a situation where

(a) You were refused permission to discuss or explore an issue? What was the result?

_____

_____

_____

_____

(b) You were given permission to explore an issue that interested you? What was the result?

_____

_____

_____

# CHAPTER SEVEN

# Ways You Win or Lose in Conversations

**Johnson:** Well, we had a good talk.
**Boswell:** Yes sir, you tossed and gored several persons.

*Boswell's Life of Johnson, Vol. (i)*

---

How often have you talked to someone and at the end of the conversation felt that you have got nowhere? How often have you been to a meeting and at the end walked out feeling it has been a waste of time? The reason is that often there has been a competitive win/lose conversation taking place. In short, neither side is willing to accept what the other side says. Instead everyone goes off in their own directions. We shall contrast this win/lose type of conversation with win/win conversation.

Therefore in this chapter we shall cover

- the basis for win/lose and win/win conversations

- what parallel and sequential conversations mean

- how to influence the direction of conversation

---

We shall look at the reasons and factors that influence whether or not we have a win/win or win/lose conversation by examining parallel and sequential conversations. It is possible to influence the direction of such discussions if you can identify quickly what is happening and move to correct it.

## Win/Win and Win/Lose Conversations

None of us likes to lose. Usually we take pride in not losing, although we try to exercise some grace when we do. This is difficult in conversations where there is a win/lose element.

Those who start off with the 'I bet you' approach are competitive conversationalists. They make it clear right from the beginning that they are out to win. Many people do not make it quite so obvious, but in terms of the conversation it becomes clear that they will insist upon winning at the expense of other people losing. However, all conversations do not need to be that way. There is an opportunity in most conversations for people to establish situations where both sides can get something out of it. It is generally understood that the most effective conversations are those where both sides come away feeling that they have gained something from the meeting.

Figure 7.1 illustrates the four major options that we have in any conversation.

ME

|  |  | Lose | Win |
|---|---|---|---|
| YOU | Lose | Both lose | I win – You lose |
|  | Win | You win – I lose | Both win |

FIGURE 7.1  *The win/lose conversational model*

**Option A.** *I win – you lose.* Here I arrange the conversation so that I get across my points in such a way that I gain from the conversation and you feel, as a result, that you have lost. In such a situation I will feel that I have obtained a plus and you will feel you have obtained a minus. Unless you acknowledge that what you are trying to achieve is wrong, then you are likely to go away frustrated and annoyed.

**Option B.** *You win – I lose.* Here I feel that, in the conversation, you have managed to get the better of me. As a consequence you will feel that you have come out of the meeting with a plus. So I will probably be irritable, annoyed and frustrated and may have a desire to gain revenge at our next meeting, when I will want to win at your expense.

**Option C.** *I lose – you lose.* Here is a situation where we have a

70

discussion and both of us make it impossible for the other to win. We even go further than this. We make sure that each other loses. In such cases we both feel we come out of the meeting with a minus. We will both feel equally annoyed and disappointed but perhaps secretly pleased that we prevented the other person from winning, despite our own loss. Too often union/management confrontations can end up where both sides lose because neither is prepared to give way.

**Option D.** *I win – you win.* This is the ideal situation in all conversations. We both end up with a feeling of having gained something from the meeting. The person who exercises conversational control will ensure that the other person gains something from the meeting, however small. To go away with nothing is invariably a loss of face. Therefore the skilled conversationalist will look for opportunities to facilitate the win/win situation. This is particularly necessary in situations where people must work together over a period.

I was impressed by the comment made by a general secretary of the British Trades Union Congress, when he said '90 per cent or more of the issues I have been involved in have been resolved in the end with a form of words. Usually the nature of what is acceptable about those words is such that you don't talk too much about defeat and victory' (Willis, 1984).

The emphasis must be on problem-solving rather than winning or losing when negotiating and discussing issues with people with whom we are going to have a long-term relationship. However, every conversation, discussion and negotiation cannot end in a win/win situation. But in terms of conversation control we should gauge our contributions to achieve an objective which enables subsequent discussions to take place without the basic motivation being recrimination and revenge. Therefore, even when you do win, ensure the other side goes away with something to maintain self-respect.

# Ways in Which You Can Go for the Win/Win

If you decide that it is important for the other person or other side to gain something from the conversation, try to find out what they regard as the key issues. To do this you must clearly use your requesting skills and work on the problem-centred part of the circle. You need to do this while making it clear through your statements and solution-centred behaviour what you want. In this way you can move to joint problem-solving.

I find it easier to move towards a win/win conversation by putting the key points on to a blackboard or some form of visual aid. This enables the matters to be resolved in such a way that both sides can have their concerns discussed thoroughly. List the points people raise even if you disagree with them.

A good example of this occurred recently at a presentation made by a consultant to senior managers about a new training course. Initially the managers were hostile to the proposals. They threw lots of objections forward, seeking a win/lose confrontation where they could prove the consultant wrong. The consultant, instead of countering each statement, put each point onto a visual aid and asked questions. When the managers responded, he answered with facts where appropriate and showed concern for the feelings expressed. Gradually the tone of the conversation changed to joint problem-solving and a win/win atmosphere developed. The consultant agreed to amend the programme according to the points raised. The managers recognized that they had influenced the outcome to achieve the points they wanted. Good conversation control can lead to win/win situations when both sides behave in an appropriate fashion.

# Parallel Win/Lose Conversations

The essential nature of parallel conversations is that what one person has to say does not bear much relation to what another person has said. There is a tendency for people to pursue what they want to say regardless of what the other person says. Let us look at an example.

**Person A:** It is very important that over the next few months we reduce our costs.

**Person B:** I believe that the most important thing is to increase our sales.

**Person A:** By reducing our costs we can have an immediate impact on the organization.

**Person B:** I don't like taking a negative approach to things. I believe we should go out and try to capture a wider share of the market place. This will mean increasing costs initially but will also produce bigger returns.

**Person A:** We have to go for a method which will work in the short term. Cost reduction is the only way in which we can do that.

**Person B:** I disagree. The same effort put into increasing sales can have a much bigger impact all round.

On the surface these two people seem to be having a conversation. However, they have entirely different views on how to tackle the problem, and neither is prepared to listen to what the other is saying. They are therefore pursuing parallel lines.

One person puts forward a statement. The other person then counters this with another statement. The result is that the original person reiterates his/her original position and this is then countered by the other. It is not so much a conversation as a series of statements. The result is that they talk at each other rather than *with* each other.

Parallel conversation in this particular case consists of an exchange of 'I am right' and 'you are wrong' win/lose dialogue. Neither side is interested in exploring the meaning behind the words used by the other person. No questions were asked and no further information is obtained other than the original statement.

For Person A to get his message across he feels he has not only to reiterate his point of view but become more extreme in stating it. Likewise Person B, to get his point across, feels that to listen to the other person will be showing interest in a direction that he does not wish to take.

In real life this may be a perfectly acceptable position to take. If you do not wish to take an interest in the other's views and ideas, but just wish to reiterate your own position, then it is no use pretending to do otherwise.

Parallel conversation in a non-win/lose format is, however, the way to go if you want to develop a lot of creative ideas. Brainstorming is a technique where people develop lots of ideas on a problem as a first stage without anyone criticizing the ideas, and is a particularly effective way of quickly generating options. In one sense it is not really a conversation but a structured way of getting people to contribute solutions.

Parallel conversation in a group or large meeting can end up in a series of statements and speeches where everyone talks and no one really listens. I have termed this the conversational parcel game. Here each person unfolds an agenda and talks to it for a few minutes. The next speaker then speaks to another agenda and so on. Each speaker has brought a parcel, which is opened, but little or no interest is shown in other people's parcels.

Conversational parcels is also played when a person comments on another's contribution, only to knock it down in favour of his own proposition. We have all seen this form of parallel conversation in Parliament or Congress during political debates. There are two major kinds of win/lose parallel conversations. One is called the polarization effect and the other the fixation effect. See Figures 7.2 and 7.3 (Margerison, 1974).

FIGURE 7.2   *The polarization effect*

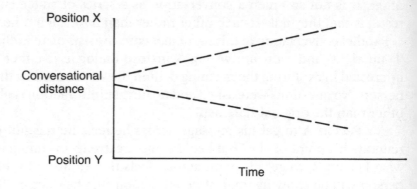

This, as can be seen, means that you get further apart as you talk. Where the two parties in a problem-solving meeting insist on the correctness of their own position, refuse to listen to each other's comments, criticize each other's statements, and seek to prove the superiority of their own position, then polarization will occur. The interpersonal problem-solving distance will increase, and the gap between the parties will be wider at the conclusion of the meeting than at the beginning.

If you wish to prevent polarization taking place, seek to move the conversation on to a sequential basis by summarizing, asking questions, building on what has been said and linking your responses to the other person's comments. If, however, you wish to highlight the differences or go for a 'win/lose' conversation, then be assertive and put forward your views strongly, spelling out clearly the way in which they differ from your opponent's. If you wish to polarize the conversation, make sure you have a firm position, based not just on your beliefs but also on the facts.

FIGURE 7.3 *The fixation effect*

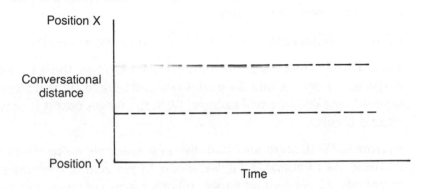

Both parties here take up fixed positions and conduct a meeting which reinforces their original differences. Neither side is prepared to give way; neither side generates new information; neither side takes up new opinions.

Figure 7.3 illustrates a rather boring conversation. It sounds like a broken record going over the same worn-out tune. The fixation conversation is probably played most often in family life, where those who live with each other have routine differences which they repeat. Everyone knows the other's position, but they keep on hammering away on such matters as getting the children to clean their rooms or politics. No one will change. Fixation has set in. The same can occur at work.

## Sequential Win/Win Conversation

If you feel that there may be something worthwhile in what the other person says, it is important to develop a sequential conversation. If we go back to the original example we can see how a person who is interested in developing a sequential conversation could control the conversation in order to facilitate this. In essence, a sequential conversation is one in which there is some link between what one person says with what the other person says, so that over a period of time thoughts and ideas are developed in a pattern.

In the example below Person B develops a sequence of conversation based on what Person A has to say and then links this to his own ideas.

**Person A:** I believe it's important that we reduce costs if we are to make the organisation more effective.

**Person B:** What costs in particular did you have in mind?

**Person A:** The most important costs that we have are those for materials and wages. I believe that if we sat down and looked at the materials cost we could make some real savings. With the wages cost it is obviously more difficult.

**Person B:** Well, there are about five key materials we use in our business. As I understand it, we spend 35 per cent of our budget on chemicals, 25 per cent on paper and other forms of raw material, 20 per cent on machine parts and 10 per cent each on office materials and factory accessories. Where could we make the biggest impact?

**Person A:** Well, it's years since we looked at how we buy chemicals, for example. I also believe that the way we use them in the factory could be vastly improved. There must also be other savings elsewhere.

**Person B:** Let's call together all those people who use these materials and see what we can do.

**Person A:** That's a good idea. I think it might be useful to have a task force working on the matter.

**Person B:** We should also look at how we can increase our sales.

**Person A:** Yes, but costs are the most important thing and we should concentrate on those first.

**Person B:** I believe that through the task force we can do this and get some quick results. In addition, we can use the same approach to improving our sales.

**Person A:** Yes, if it works on costs, there is no reason it can't work on increasing sales also.

That is a conversation designed clearly to show how the ideas of one person are considered and built upon by the other in a sequential way. Person B clearly listens for what Person A has to say and asks questions to draw out the key points underlying the initial statements. Once Person B has done this, he also summarizes his understanding of what the other person has said.

There are two major forms of sequential conversation – the persuasian effect and the co-operation effect. See Figures 7.4 and 7.5.

FIGURE 7.4  *Persuasion effect*

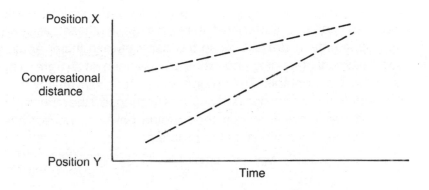

In this type of problem-solving meeting there is not only agreement, but both parties move in the direction of the position held by one of them. The characteristics of this form of meeting are that people are prepared to listen, to be flexible, to judge on evidence, not to be bound by prejudice, and to risk taking up new attitudes and behaviour. There is clearly a win/ lose element but it is based on a mutual understanding that this is the best way to go. Usually such a meeting is a sequential one where there is an attempt to understand, recognize and appreciate each person's position. Each person will lead and follow accordingly in ordor to solve the problem

# Know the Direction in Which You are Going

All conversations are moving either towards you, away from you or against you. Think of any recent conversation you have had and assess

FIGURE 7.5  *The co-operation effect*

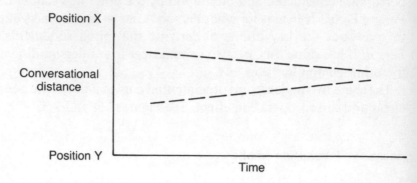

Here both parties are prepared to listen to each other's case and, where appropriate, take steps to close the gap between them. Again there is some element of winning and losing but it is done on an agreed basis and is mutually acceptable. The co-operation effect is invariably the function of a negotiation where one party agrees to change if the other will do so. To this end, both move away from their original positions, but achieve a basis for agreement and action on the problem.

how the other person or people reacted to you based on what I have called the conversation direction chart (Figure 7.6).

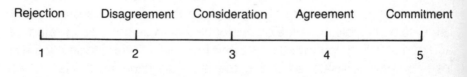

FIGURE 7.6  *Conversation direction chart*

In each meeting people will react to what you have to say in one of the five ways shown in Figure 7.6. Clearly the more you are to the left, the more you will have a parallel or even divergent conversation; and the more you are to the right, the more you will have a sequential conversation.

1.  *Rejection*. This is an outright refusal to go any further with either a

request or a statement on the opinion, information, or action under discussion.

2. *Disagreement.* This is a denial of the proposition put forward, but contains a willingness to continue the discussion.

3. *Consideration.* This is a point at which a person is willing to think about a request or statement, but not accept or reject the other's opinion, knowledge, or action until more is known.

4. *Agreement.* This is an expression of accord, whereby one person accepts the validity of the other's opinion, knowledge, or action.

5. *Commitment.* This is where a decision on the substance of the opinions, knowledge, and actions reflects itself in a commitment to implementing the decision.

Your conversation control skills will determine how successful you are in moving your discussions and meetings to the right-hand side of the scale. Here people will not only agree but be committed to working with you to implement a decision.

# How to Manage Disagreement and Rejection

You need to practise how to recognize the opposite reaction quickly and how to cope with disagreement and rejection. Some tactics for coping with rejection and disagreement are:

- summarizing the conversation so far and asking the other person if your summary is accurate

- then asking the other person what would be required for them to change their view

- listening carefully for the cues and clues and particularly any expressions of feeling and concern

- indicating you understand, recognize and appreciate their concerns in a genuine manner

- outlining what, if anything, you can and will do to help meet those concerns.

The steps should ensure you are at least talking about the real reasons for disagreement and rejection. It will usually mean you have a sound problem-solving discussion, but not that everyone will suddenly agree with you. The first step is to get to consider what you are saying.

These models in Figures 7.2 and 7.6 are useful in providing us with a visual pattern of what is happening in a conversation. The important thing is to chart the direction of conversation in your head so that you can move them in the direction you want to take them rather than letting them drift.

# Guidelines

In most discussions problem-solving can occur through sequential conversation, where one person listens and builds upon what the other says. The result is that when you then express your views, the other person is more willing to listen. The 'unwritten contract' usually implies: 'If you are prepared to listen to me then I am prepared to listen to you'.

However, it requires one person to take the initiative in conversational control. In this case we have shown that, through the use of sequential conversation, it is possible to move towards problem-solving dialogue by establishing co-operation between people rather than just an exchange of statements as to who is right and who is wrong.

Sequential conversation control is a skill that can be learnt and built into day-to-day conversational principles and practices. It demands respect for what others say and considering their viewpoint before reaching a judgement. It should, if used appropriately, lead to more win/win conversations.

Beware, however, of parallel meetings that degenerate into the opening of many conversational parcels, none of which are sufficiently explored, and people go away dissatisfied. Ensure you identify the key 'parcels' and indicate that each one of them needs to be discussed in turn. Then introduce an order of priority into the discussion. This is the way to use a parallel conversation for maximum benefit. It happens, for example, in brainstorming meetings, when the aim is to generate as many ideas as possible.

In summary it is useful to have parallel conversations where:

- you want to present a point of view and hear the other person's position

- creative ideas are being sought and the exchange of different approaches is welcome

- negotiation is at a particular stage

It is useful to have sequential conversations when you are:

- trying to understand in depth someone's thoughts

- trying to solve problems

- aiming to build and develop a conversation in a particular area

Decide what kind of conversation you wish to achieve. If it is a win/win objective, try to develop a persuasion or co-operation effect. If you feel you must try and win your case at the expense of others, then go for a polarization effect to highlight the differences.

# Exercises

1.  What would you do if, as a chairperson of a meeting, you recognized that you had people in the group who were playing conversational parcels and conducting parallel conversations?

_____

_____

2.  What would you say to develop a sequential conversation in the following situation?

    **You:** I think we should press on quickly and send a notice out to everyone telling them they will be scheduled to attend a two-day briefing on our new appraisal system.

**Colleague:** I disagree. That sounds too much like the military where everyone is given orders to attend. The important thing here is to get a high level of co-operation and motivation.

_____

_____

_____

_____

3.  Consider the meetings you have had recently and identify what kind they were and what happened.

(a) Persuasion meeting _____

_____

(b) Co-operation meeting _____

_____

(c) Fixation meeting _____

_____

(d) Polarization meeting _____

_____

# CHAPTER EIGHT

# How to use Facts and Opinions to Diverge and Converge

'I disapprove of what you say, but I will defend to the death your right to say it.'

*Voltaire*

Facts and opinions are the life blood of all conversations. It is impossible to have a conversation without incorporating facts and opinions. It is important to know how to manage conversations in order to gain the benefit from the facts and opinions available to help solve problems. In this chapter the following will be covered:

- how to gather and use facts and opinions

- how to open up and close down a conversation

- how to diverge and converge

Every day we are engaged in the exchange of facts and opinions. We depend on our ability to use facts and opinions in order to get what we want.

This is so in all our jobs but particularly so for those in police work and medicine. It is the police's job to acquire the facts that will support or refute allegations made against people, the doctors' to separate the opinions supplied by the patients from the facts related to the symptoms. However, facts without opinions rarely take us very far, especially in managerial work. To give leadership and direction managers must acquire and present the facts to support their opinions, and also develop opinions and views on what to do when the facts are there.

Most of the time we mix facts and opinions. We might, for example, cite a fact, then, as a result, express an opinion. For example, 'Our competitors have reduced their price by 10 per cent; therefore we have got to reduce our costs'. The initial statement is one of fact, the second one of opinion.

Sometimes people put their opinions first and follow up with the facts, as in this example. 'I have felt for a long time that we spend more advertising our old product, because it still costs only half that of the new product to produce.'

## Managing the Facts

A key conversational skill is to know the difference between an opinion and a fact, and to use it to your advantage. Never let a person get away by giving a set of opinions without you asking for some supporting facts. Equally never let a person confuse you with facts when what you want is an opinion on the information.

One of the world's most successful businessmen, Harold Geneen, Chairman and Chief Executive of the American giant AT and T, knew the difference between facts and opinions. Each month he would call all his senior managers together for a reporting session. At these meetings each manager had to present both facts and opinions on the state of their business operations and indicate the likely consequences. Geneen was renowned for insisting on opinions either based on or supported by what he called 'the unshakeable facts'. He once sent a memo to all his executives which read as follows: 'The highest art of professional management requires the literal ability of "smell" a "real fact" from all others – and moreover to have the temerity, intellectual curiosity, guts and/or plain impoliteness if necessary to be sure that what you do have is indeed what we will call an "unshakeable fact"' (Geneen and Moscow, 1984).

However, facts without opinions are like a car without a driver. They will not take you very far. You need to be able to drive your facts by having opinions and views on what they mean. There are various stages in which you need to develop skills. First establish why you want facts, then proceed as follows:

1.  *Gather the facts*. It is not always easy to recognize a fact even when it is presented. The speed of presentation and the number of facts available may make it difficult for us to understand. Therefore, unless you have a clear purpose, you may not understand what facts

are important. Learn how to get the essential information on to paper or on to a visual aid. Develop a shorthand way of recording the data, so that you can refer to it easily.

2. *Understand the facts.* If the facts are not clear to you, then start asking some questions. They may be general open-ended questions such as 'How did you obtain this information?' or more specific questions such as 'Why is it that the figures you gave at the beginning are not in line with the final results you have outlined?' Or you may simply wish to say 'Thank you for all the information you have presented; what in your opinion does it mean?' So understanding can be a matter of clarifying the facts or appreciating the meaning behind the facts. So far you have not moved to the important stage of using the facts.

3. *Use the facts and opinions.* To use facts you need to have an opinion on what can and should be done. At this point you are going beyond what is known. This is a key point in business. You can do all the market research studies and have a myriad of financial calculations but they will be of little value unless your opinion, on which these studies have been conducted, is sound.

## Using Generals and Specifics in Conversation

As we use facts and opinions, we do so either in a general or specific way in order to make our point. Conversations take place at various levels. It is important to know how to convert generalities to specifics and when to move from specific issues to general principles. You can find out more and communicate more by knowing how to manage general and specific aspects of conversation.

Being able to muster facts and opinions in conversation is the basis for having influence and persuasion. I saw this clearly in a brilliant sales demonstration, one of the best I have ever heard. The result was that I bought something that previously I did not realize I needed – a new shower rose.

The salesman was a master of moving from the general to the specific. As I walked by his stall at a trade fair, I heard him ask 'How much money do you lose when taking a shower?' He went from the general question to making the following points:

1.  'Most of us are using three times the hot water we need when we have a shower because the shower head is too big' (specific fact).

2.  'The result is you use more electricity than you need' (general fact).

These were points of general interest. Then he proceeded to show specifically what this meant. He used an old shower rose and ran the shower for 23 seconds, and a 2-gallon bucket was filled. He then used the new shower head and ran the shower for 23 seconds, and only half a gallon of water was used without reducing the effectiveness of the shower.

He then answered specific questions with specific facts in a straightforward manner. 'How much does it cost?' 'Seventy-three dollars.' 'How long does it take to fit?' 'Five minutes just by unscrewing the old one and replacing it with the new one.' 'How much does it save in electricity?' 'It cuts your bills by a third'.

So the salesman not only sold one to me but to lots of others as well. Why? Were we gullible and easily persuaded to part with seventy-three dollars?

Of course no one would have bought the product if they did not think they needed it. However, many could have walked past the salesman if he had not been skilled in conversation control. His main skill was in moving from the general to the specific and being able to show the benefits for each individual.

Having started with the general question about the cost of taking a shower, he then showed, in time and cost, the difference between an old and a new system. He converted his verbals into visuals. Then he went on to respond to specific questions with specific, factual answers.

There is a lesson here for all of us concerned with conversation control. Too many meetings fail because people do not manage their discussions between the general and specific issues well enough or build on the interest and concerns of those with whom they are talking. Therefore, in your conversation, gauge where you should be operating. The way to do this is to see the way the conversation is going. For example, based on the above discussion, the four main options are shown in Figure 8.1.

Figure 8.1 provides the basis for looking at how conversations can 'get lost' when one person is talking specific facts and the other is giving general opinions. To exercise conversational control you need to know how to move in and out of each of the areas, using the skills of opening

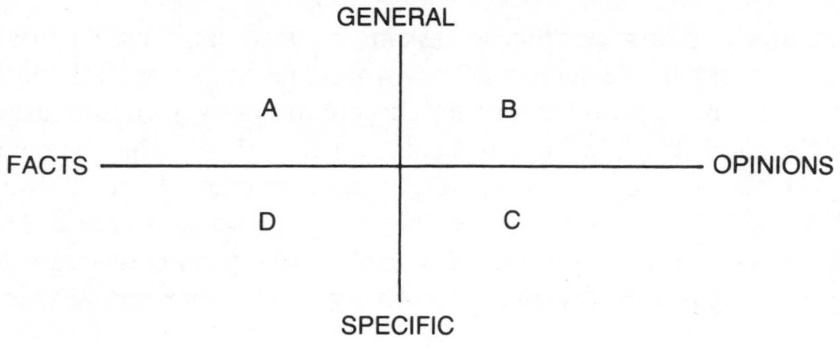

GENERAL

A          B

FACTS ——————————————————————— OPINIONS

D          C

SPECIFIC

FIGURE 8.1

up and closing down conversations, according to the diverging and converging principles. However, as George Ade wryly noted 'For parlour use the vague generality is a life saver'. From time to time in business it can do likewise – but only for a limited period.

## How to Converge and Diverge in Conversation

In daily life we move from situations where we have the facts in search of opinions or from opinions in search of facts. To be successful in conversation control you need to be able to manage both situations. The first is what we call diverging conversation and the second converging conversation.

If someone says to you 'I believe we should . . .', then it is clearly a future-orientated opinion. You may agree, but should you jump straight into action? At this point it is a good rule to ask what facts you have to back up your opinion. If you have none, start asking questions and go back to stage one of gathering the facts.

On other occasions a person will present you with facts but no more. I once had an accountant who said 'It's my job to provide the figures and explain them, not to pass opinions on what should or should not be done as a result'. He was not prepared to commit himself to either a future-based general or specific opinion on the action required.

All conversations are a combination of converging and diverging words. Those who are in need of a quick answer will want to converge quickly to find out how, when, where, why and who. Those who are

87

prepared to take more time will ask more questions, consider more ideas and not rush into a decision. They will prefer to gather all the facts and assess all the options before they commit themselves. In the hurly-burly of business this is always difficult, but it is those who through their conversation know how to diverge then converge who succeed.

We all diverge and converge. It is a key conversation control skill in the use of facts and opinions. You can improve your conversation skills by learning how to diverge and converge at the appropriate times.

## The Diverging Principle

Here you are broadening the conversation. You may have an opinion, often called a hypothesis, which you want to prove. At this point you need to gather and understand a lot of facts and ideas. You therefore move from the specific to the general. You start to diverge by comparing, sharing information and getting a wider view. Diverging is the process we use when we are searching. It is often the result of casual conversation but can be planned through brainstorming and creativity workshops.

If you are diverging you will say such things as:

'Let's look at some other ideas.'
'What do you feel about this proposal?'
'What other options do we have?'

Diverging means the conversation will roam over numerous areas. It may initially look like a parallel conversation, but as the exchange develops, threads between the various inputs should emerge.

## The Converging Principle

If you are converging you will say such things as:

'The way we tackle this is . . .'
'Let me have the report on this by Friday.'
'The time has come for us to make a decision.'
'We need to gather some specific facts to test these views.'

When you have a lot of facts, you can start making some deductions as to what they mean. In police work, for example, this is a regular procedure: clues (facts) left at the scene of a crime have to be interpreted. The police have to form specific opinions and see if the facts fit. They start to converge. So it is in business. You may have a good idea for a product but testing it out requires that, after diverging, you converge on specific applications.

# The Diverging/Converging Index

How do you see your major strengths in conversation? Are you better at diverging or converging? This exercise is a quick self-check although it does not cover all the issues. Please base your score on the scale below.

| 1 | 2 | 3 | 4 | 5 |
|---|---|---|---|---|
| Rarely | Occasionally | Sometimes | Often | Very often |

A.  I generate a lot of ideas  _____
B.  I like to get into action  _____
C.  I am good at asking open questions  _____
D.  I have an open mind on most issues  _____
E.  I like to hear other people's views  _____
F.  I like to get to the heart of the matter quickly  _____
G.  I enjoy theorizing  _____
H.  I try to get people to come to the point quickly  _____
I.  I find it hard at times to bring a discussion to a close _____
J.  I emphasize getting a conclusion  _____
K.  I don't like leaving things up in the air for too long _____
L.  I concentrate on results  _____
M.  I prefer work-specific conversation to social discussions  _____
N.  I prefer opinions to facts  _____

Allocate the scores you have chosen to each of the letters below.

|  | Diverging items |  | Converging items |
|---|---|---|---|
| A | _____ | B | _____ |
| C | _____ | F | _____ |
| D | _____ | H | _____ |
| E | _____ | J | _____ |
| G | _____ | K | _____ |
| I | _____ | L | _____ |
| N | _____ | M | _____ |
|  | _____ |  | _____ |

Total

If you score less than 20 on the diverging scale, you need to practise your conversation control skills for open-ended questions, and propose new ideas and listen without rushing to conclusions. If you score under 20 on converging, start to monitor your use of time in conversation and learn how to get to the point more quickly.

# Guidelines

It is important for a manager to distinguish between facts and opinions. The following are some useful rules:

1.  Having stated the problem, collect the available facts from everyone.

2.  When people give opinions, ask them what evidence they have to back them up.

3.  When people give facts, ask them what they feel are the implications, so that they also give opinions.

4.  When one person gives a fact or an opinion that others find hard to respond to, ask them how they feel about it.

5.  When people exhibit strong feelings, first of all summarize in their own words what they have said, then ask them for the facts underlying their views.

In using these approaches you can begin to find a balance between facts and opinions. You will become a link person in the conversation, guiding people to talk with each other in a problem-solving way. The alternative often results in people having a parallel conversation, just making statements to each other. Here no one follows on, nor links what they are saying to what other people have said.

You can develop your ability to open up and close down a conversation by diverging and converging.

To diverge you can:

- introduce an open-ended question

- ask for ideas

- put forward some options

- indicate by comparison other ways of doing things

- request a different approach

To converge you can:

- propose a deadline

- indicate a specific line of action

- ask for specific facts

- allocate roles, duties and accountability

# Exercise

The difficulty is that facts and opinions often get mixed up in such a way that conversations get out of control. Quite simply people either do not obtain or give the facts, or put their opinions in an unacceptable form. How would you try to maintain conversation control if you were John Brent in this case?

John Brent is a production manager in a large manufacturing organization. He has been concerned for some time that production has been below budget. He decides therefore to call together the five immediate supervisors who report to him, to discuss the reasons for the poor performance. He also invites the personnel manager. In the conversation below, *identify those people who speak on the basis of facts or opinions* and try to decide whether or not they are exercising conversation control.

**John Brent:** As you know, for the last couple of months we have not been able to meet our budget on production. For 6 out of the 8 weeks we have been 10 per cent below the budget and for the last 2 weeks we have been 20 per cent below. I felt it would be useful if we discussed what was causing the problem and worked out some ways of tackling it.

**Supervisor A:** As I see it, the reason for the problem is quite simple. As we know, at the moment we have an absenteeism rate of between 10 and 20 per cent most weeks of the year. On average 10 per cent of the available work time is wasted on a breakdown of at least one machine. Both these factors will stop us achieving our budget.

**Supervisor B:** I disagree. We made some assumptions on both breakdowns and absenteeism when we created the budget. In my view it's just a simple matter of getting people to do what they're supposed to do. I believe that we should be more strict with the staff, particularly with tea breaks, and tell them either to perform or move on.

**Supervisor C:** If you ask me, the budget is the problem. We should never have accepted the outputs and the costs in the first place. There is no way with the existing staff and resources that we can regularly achieve those budgets.

**Supervisor A:** I would agree. Look at the machinery that we have here. There is not one machine that is less than 8 years old. No wonder they're always breaking down.

**Supervisor C:** Although the machines are old, I find that there is no problem in getting them to run at 100 per cent of their capacity when they are working. My view is that what we really need is a good bonus system to get people motivated.

**Personnel Manager:** I've interviewed a number of people over the last year who have left to try to find out what they see as the key problems. The labour turnover rate in this department is currently running at 30 per cent, which is twice the average for the factory as a whole. Those who leave tell me that they did not enjoy working in the department because of the pressure exerted on them by supervisors.

**Supervisor A:** That's a load of rubbish! Anyone who leaves the organization is going to make some pathetic excuse. You're so gullible, you believe everything they say. It's about time you started listening to us and not them.

**Personnel Manager:** I'm only telling you exactly what those who leave actually say.

The meeting has not been going very long and yet already a number of facts and opinions are beginning to show. The manager, John Brent, will now have the task of trying to exert some direction and influence over the meeting. How should he manage the general and specific views expressed? Should he concentrate on the facts or should he try to draw out people's opinions more clearly? Should he encourage people to diverge more or should he get them to converge on specific aspects? These are options which every manager has to face in any meeting. What would your strategy be in this situation?

# CHAPTER NINE

# How Visuals can Improve your Verbals

'Language is the dress of thought.'

Samuel Johnson, *Lives of the English Poets*

---

We retain about 80 per cent of what we see, but only 20 per cent of what we hear, and most meetings are dominated by verbals rather than visuals. With practice, however, we can all improve our problem-solving abilities by improving our use of visuals in conversation. The visuals can be in the form of metaphors, similes or analogies as well as tangible visual aids.

We shall therefore cover:

- the relation of verbals to visuals

- how to make visual summaries

- the value of word pictures

- the way words on our face and fingers actually work

---

The problem with words is that we have heard most, if not all, of them before. You have to do something special with words if you want to gain people's attention. You may change the tone of your voice to emphasize a point, use strong words or stress the important consequences to the listener of what you have to say. Nevertheless words often fall like water off the duck's back and there is little to see for your efforts.

As we all spend so much time talking, it is therefore worthwhile to consider how we can be more effective in our conversation. The first thing to note is that research evidence tells us that visual material has on average a longer lasting impact on us than mere words. Given that we are surrounded by visual media these days, it is important that we recognize the way people are conditioned to visual imagery, and expect us to illustrate what we have to say in some equally meaningful visual way.

For some people this is easy. Such people think in pictures. Artists, for example, have a well tuned visual appreciation of a person or situation, and can represent what they see, not in words but in drawings. Accountants can usually do the same by representing the day-to-day activities of business in a pattern of figures. Architects can take your half-formed ideas and develop a design for your house. The art or skill of visualizing what we talk about is built into the training of some professional groups. I believe it needs to be more specifically built into the training of managers with particular reference to conversation control.

There are many forms of visual expression in conversation, including the use of visual aids, the creation of word pictures, and gestures and gesticulations. We shall start by returning to the John Brent case and look at one option that he could have adopted: using a visual aid as part of his team problem-solving effort.

# How to Convert Verbals to Visuals

The meeting between John Brent and his colleagues in the exercise section of the last chapter is a good example of the need to convert verbal contributions into a visual form. He called the meeting on an important topic and asked people to give their views. He received the normal expressions of facts and opinions.

In John Brent's case he could, before the meeting, have circulated a document outlining the problem and given some facts to stress its seriousness. He could have then asked other people to do some homework, and write down information before the meeting which could have then been circulated.

Therefore at the meeting, instead of people just putting forward facts and opinions 'off the top of their heads', they could have talked in a more organized way, using documents covering key points which had been assessed beforehand. In this way John Brent would have had an influence on conversation control at the meeting by getting people to refer to documents that made visible not only the problem but also the options and alternatives they could consider. By producing the visuals he would have made an impact on the problem-solving process.

John Brent did not do this. He held a meeting in which lots of facts and opinions were expressed in a disorganized way. The danger of this is that people put forward views which are either not heard by other people or are forgotten. When this occurs, there is a tendency for people to repeat themselves, as shown in this short extract from the meeting.

**Supervisor A:** As I said before, unless we come to terms with the fact that we have up to 20 per cent absenteeism and machine breakdowns on average of up to 10 per cent, we're not going to do anything. This, to me, is the main issue we have to address.

**Supervisor C:** Yes, but even so, I still think that the budget is too high and we have to look more carefully at what we can actually expect people to produce.

**Supervisor B:** To my mind, it's a question of motivation. I tend to agree with the Personnel Manager in that we have to look at the way in which we are managing the staff.

**Supervisor A:** I won't be happy until we look more closely at the cause of machine breakdowns and why people are absent 20 per cent of the time.

Clearly in this conversation the members are beginning to repeat themselves. No one is prepared to discuss the other person's view until his own agenda item has been registered and acknowledged as an important issue for discussion. Unless John Brent does something about this, he is likely to have a meeting which quickly gets out of control.

When this happens, it is useful for the manager to have the skill of being able to visualize what the issues are. Instead of letting the verbal exchange dominate the meeting, John Brent has to introduce the visual dimension.

This is easily done if he has a board or a flip-chart in the meeting room, together with some marker pens. At this stage of the meeting it would be helpful for him to write on the board the key points emerging from the diverging part of the discussion which people see as factors needing to be dealt with to cope with the decline in production. John Brent should therefore go to the board and make a list that includes the following items:

* machine breakdowns
* absenteeism

- staff timekeeping – tea breaks

- age of machines

- budget – cost and output targets

- bonus system

- managerial style

- pay

'These are, as I see them,' John Brent said, 'the major points that people have raised in the meeting so far. It might be useful if we could discuss each of these and see what we can do to improve the situation.'

Providing he has accurately summarized the issues raised by the members, it is probable that they will no longer have to reiterate their particular points, or attack somebody else's point in order to get theirs heard. Moreover, by having the issues in a visual form, people can more easily retain the complexity of the problem and converge on specific actions.

## Visual Summaries

The visual form also enables people to suggest options, to gather more facts, to assess the validity of opinions, and to provide a focus for feelings. All key points should be summarized.

A good example of the use of visuals came in a meeting I had with a board of directors of a large company. They had asked me to talk through with them their strategies and plans for the future at a meeting held off-site over a weekend. The chairman indicated at the first session that a major problem had arisen and needed to be discussed urgently. He apologized to me for not being able to address the set agenda, but asked me to stay and offer my advice on the problem. I said I would be happy to do so and help write up the main points that emerged from the discussion on the board.

I made a visual record of what was said, starting with the problem statement, the objectives, the views of each person and the options for action. After 2 hours of intense debate the chairman summed up and allocated the duties of each person prior to the next meeting. At the tea break the directors commented that it had been a most successful meeting. One senior member said 'That is the best meeting we have had all year'. When I enquired what the difference between it and the previous meetings was, he said 'We could all see what we were doing and what needs to be done. It speeded up the process of discussion and got us to the point more quickly'.

Therefore the use of visuals to chart a meeting can be helpful, whether it be in the situation confronted by John Brent or in a directors' meeting dealing with a crisis. In my experience too few managers use visual aids to identify the key points of a meeting. I have noted that only about one-quarter to one-third of managers have visual-aid facilities in their own offices. If I could make one change to improve conversation control, it would be to install a visual aid in every manager's office and give them training in its use.

## Make Word Pictures through Metaphors, Analogies and Similes

Not only can visual aids help in transforming abstract conversation into concrete ideas and solutions, but verbals can be used in such a way so as to create visuals in the listeners' minds.

We have all heard the great orators. They never just give the facts and figures. They draw word pictures. Their language is full of pertinent adjectives. They stress what they have to say with words that paint a picture. Winston Churchill, even during the darkest days of war, would converse in word pictures – 'I can promise you nothing but blood, sweat and tears'. Luther King is remembered for his speech when he pronounced 'I have a dream'. Ronald Reagan talked of the United States as 'the shining city on the hill'. The words all conjure up pictures of meaning.

Adjectives can play an important part in any conversation. They not only describe but give emphasis to the key points. Consider these two ways in which respective managers converse with their teams and see the difference in the use of word pictures. Which will be remembered for longer and which will have the greater motivational impact?

**Manager A:** Our results this year have been above average. We have done well and should be proud of our achievements. Next year will be equally demanding and I trust you will all give the same commitment.

**Manager B:** Our results this year reflect our teamwork. I don't say that lightly. We have proved we are the front runners and champions of our industry. It has been a herculean effort all round. I appreciate the tremendous commitment and support everyone has given. We've got a first division team here and I know we can press on and climb even higher peaks in the New Year.

The second manager introduces into his conversation not only adjectives but images with which people can associate. John Lennon in his song 'Imagine' had that ability. Politicians like John Kennedy, Gandhi and Lincoln captured the imagination with their words also. However, we do not have to be great orators or song-writers to make people aware of what we are saying.

Effective communicators in business are able to conjure a picture through their use of words. They also simplify a complex problem. For example, sales managers often take sporting or military analogies to make what they have to say more graphic. They will refer to 'the sales campaign' as 'a battle we must win'. The specific sporting analogies often relate 'to teamwork and scoring more goals than the opposition'.

Some people find it easy to talk in word pictures. They seem to have a store of visual images drawn from a wide variety of situations. These can include such examples as:

- nursery rhymes – 'Humpty Dumpty' when things are falling apart

- the Bible – 'David and Goliath' struggles or 'Prophets in their own land'

- books – *Sherlock Holmes* analogies for investigations

- sport – analogies of teams and individuals winning and losing

- stories – heroes and villains

- wars – reference to battles and victory

People often give advice in word pictures such as: 'put your shoulder to the wheel' or 'step on the gas'. They reflect danger in word pictures when they talk about the possibility of 'falling between two stools'. Often people can be critical or sarcastic by graphically referring to someone who is mean as having 'short arms and long pockets'. Sometimes the metaphors can be quite funny, such as the comment about one manager's approach to not taking action: 'He's too scared to put his toe in the water'. Another manager quickly added 'He would be out of his depth if he did'.

Dale Carnegie in his works on personal influence indicated that it is important to talk in pictures and get people to identify with what you are saying. Therefore, when it is appropriate, use metaphors, similes and analogies. You can train yourself to think and talk in word pictures. You need to collect examples and illustrations which you can draw upon. Try, where possible, to identify with the interests of the person with whom you are speaking. For example, if the person likes sailing, you can use metaphors like 'getting into deep water' or 'sailing too close to the wind' to reinforce your concerns. If the person is a golfer, you may refer to 'having a difficult lie' if things are tough. You need first to recognize what the other person will be interested in, then build your word picture to their interests.

# Make Use of Verbal Shorthand

We have developed ways of shortening our communication through common terms and phrases which we assume everyone else understands. Each of these is culture-bound and often not understood by people from overseas. For example, the term 'Taking coals to Newcastle' is one which is often used in business situations to indicate that there is no point in trying to market a product to an area or customers who are already well supplied by people in that market place. The use of the phrase in itself is not particularly meaningful unless everyone understands the context and cultural background. Much conversation control depends on using such metaphors and analogies at the appropriate time, in order to have maximum effectiveness.

'I believe we are putting all our eggs in one basket' said a senior manager at one meeting when objecting to a proposal to concentrate the money for new product development into a particular area. Again this is a clear example of using verbal shorthand to get at a key issue. Later in the conversation another manager responded by saying 'It's no use putting a bet on every horse in the race, we have got to concentrate our resources on what we think will be the winners'. Here again was another useful piece of verbal shorthand which clearly made the point.

My own view is that verbal shorthand is a key to success in conversational control. Those people who can talk in analogies and metaphors, and begin to paint a word picture to such illustrations, can often begin to have an impact. Although the points they are making are general ones,

101

people are able to identify with the general theme rather than the specific argument. Clearly one has to back up one's analogies and metaphors with facts and figures. However, to get the point across in the first place it is very useful to be able to use verbal shorthand as a way of communicating quickly and effectively in order to illustrate the key issues. In short, 'a wink is as good as a nod when it's six of one and half a dozen of the other . . .'

Therefore train yourself to use metaphors to emphasize and drive home a key point. Various leaders have done so. Most notably the late Premier Khrushchev did so when he said you could not 'make an omelette without breaking an egg'. President Nixon is remembered for his notorious statement 'there is no whitewash at the White House'. The visual imagery makes the point even if it is not always either true or accurate.

## The Words on Our Face and Fingers

We all show our feelings on issues by the way we look and react. This has been referred to as body language. We tend to lean forward, hand on chin when we are interested, or turn away when disinterested. Our hands and arms can indicate we are open to what is being said by being relaxed, or show that we are not by being clenched or crossed. We are therefore making body pictures of what we feel and think all the time.

Indeed people who are talking to us can often get as much information from our body posture as from what we say or how we say it. We might talk calmly but show we are anxious by moving from foot to foot or by blushing. It is hard to control one's behavioural reaction, for it is more of a stimulus response reaction than the words we use.

Nevertheless through training it is feasible to portray the image you want to others. With the advent of television as a major political medium there is a a lot of effort going into grooming representatives of organizations and particularly chief executives to control their gestures and gesticulations. All this may sound as if you need to be a good actor in order to be successful at conversation control.

The answer is, in one sense, you do. There is no use in saying one thing and doing another. The actual visual behaviour of shaking your head, for example, while saying yes will deafen the words. Those who are effective at conversation control act in a congruent way. Their behaviour matches their words. You can see they mean what they say. They present an authentic picture because their visuals match their verbals.

## How to Control Your Gestures and Gesticulations

With practice it is possible to improve your performance in conversation without adding any more words. The improvement can come because you improve your visual gestures and gesticulations. For example, you can encourage another person by smiling when he/she says something that pleases you. Indeed the smile is a very powerful gesture. It can switch people 'on and off' if done at the appropriate time.

Psychologists refer to the laws of conditioning and reinforcement. To be skilled in conversational control you need to know and apply these laws. Conditioning means having an effect on someone's behaviour by introducing a condition that either encourages or discourages that behaviour. For example, we have all been conditioned to stop when we see a red light at a traffic intersection, and to proceed if we see a green light. People can be conditioned in conversation by such visual cues.

For example, if you want someone to continue talking, smile and nod at regular intervals. The smile sets up the green light permission as a condition for the other person to speak. The nod reinforces what is being said and gives the unspoken permission to continue. People are very sensitive to such permission cues and clues. If you stop smiling and head nodding, they will usually stop and you can then contribute.

Likewise you can influence the attention of people with whom you are talking by the way you use your eyes and hands, particularly when you are addressing a group. To exercise control it is important to make eye contact with one or more people. If it is a group, move your eye contact from time to time so that each person is being conditioned to the fact that it could be their turn next for you to speak to them.

Body language and the gestures and gesticulations you make are key aspects of conversation control. Many books have been written on the subject of how our body very often tells others what we are thinking before we have spoken. The visual clues get through much more quickly than the verbal ones.

Also use your hands to emphasize a point or get them to direct the listeners' gaze where you want it to concentrate. The pointed finger or the open palm tell the story.

Our task is to line up what we say with what we do and vice versa. If you do clench your fist and are angry, then your words should reflect this. If you are relaxed, happy and smiling, then say so, or, more importantly, if you see someone else in the same state, tell them you have noted it, as this will usually reinforce what they feel. You will go up in their rating because they assess you as a positive reinforcement of their state of mind.

The same applies if you see someone is unhappy. Again, if it is appropriate, say so. It will usually facilitate discussion on a problem and the other person will warm to you for being a quick observer of their concern. In this way conversation control emerges from the visual behaviour that you observe.

So comments like 'You look well (or happy or nicely dressed)' can provide a positive base to conversations. Equally comments like 'You look sad (unhappy, concerned, worried)' can be the start of a valuable problem-solving discussion. Pay attention to the visual cues and clues that people send and build on them to establish meaningful and useful conversations.

# Guidelines

Converting verbals into visuals will not always immediately solve a problem, but is a method of helping people move the conversation on in a more positive way than just sitting exchanging verbal blows. As a start each manager therefore needs to have a visual aid blackboard or whiteboard in his/her office. Thereafter you need the confidence to be able to put on to the board the key issues, and have other people contribute, not only in a verbal way but also in a visual way.

By using the visual form both before the meeting, for preparation so that the appropriate documents can be seen at the meeting, and also during the meeting, as a way of converting words to the visual form, managers can often speed up discussions and get an overall positive result in a more effective manner. Remember, convert verbals into visuals as a key step in the problem-solving process.

Please note the following:

1. Visuals are helpful when a problem is complex. People need to *see* the facts and developments in order to build upon them.

2.  Visuals can speed up problem-solving, as people will tend not to repeat themselves if their point has been recorded.

3.  Introducing adjectives, metaphors and analogies into your conversation will make your words 'come alive' – your verbals will help visualize the issues and carry more meaning for the listener.

4.  When you are in a meeting that is not going well, it is useful to change the configuration by asking someone to outline the views with a diagram or model.

The balance between verbals and visuals in a meeting is crucial. Too often people fail to reach a decision because they mismanage the information. The movement of verbals to visuals can help improve this.

Beyond this, remember the visuals you create in your body language often speak louder than words. Congruence between what you say and what you do is vital. If it is not there, the listeners will not believe you.

All the time the visuals you create are part of the conditioning and reinforcement process. You are either encouraging people or discouraging them. Your body language is a powerful factor in conversation control. The open palm, the wagging finger, the smile and head nod or the clenched fist all tell their tale well ahead of the words.

# Exercises

1.  You have to chair a meeting which you know will be difficult because your departmental managers will be asked to cut their budgets on average by 15 per cent, owing to a fall in sales. You want to maintain their motivation and commitment during the difficult period, which could last up to a year. What metaphors, analogies or similes could help draw word pictures and help you make the points about costs containment, job quality, keeping to schedules and motivation?

_____

_____

_____

2.  You have been asked to make a speech to students at a local high school to give them information on a career in management. You recognize that a speech may be a bit dull, so you decide to introduce some visuals – both words and pictures – to accompany your talk. What would be the key visuals you would introduce?

    _____

    _____

    _____

    _____

3.  How would you describe the following, using a metaphor or analogy?

(a) Your job

    _____

(b) Your organization

    _____

(c) Your team

    _____

(d) Your last meeting

    _____

(e) Your career

    _____

# CHAPTER TEN

# Get your Summarizing Act Together

'The most fluent talkers or most plausible reasoners are not always the justest thinkers.'

William Hazlitt, *Sketches and Essays On Prejudice*

Is it possible to understand others' points of view without necessarily agreeing with them or judging them? The answer is yes. It is very important to indicate that you do understand those points of view before you judge or criticize them, or seek to express your view. A difference of opinion can lead to an outright conflict, an argument, or be resolved through problem-solving. This chapter examines how to understand before judging.

To do this we cover:

- the benefits of summarizing

- ways of summarizing

- the value of recognizing, appreciating and understanding

## The Skill of Summarizing

If I had to choose the one most important conversation control skill, I would select the skill of summarizing. To me it is the centrepiece of all conversation. Without accurate and meaningful summaries we will not improve our understanding. In order to have conversations from which we gain benefit we need to practise our summarizing skills.

We are not talking here of mere parroting what the other person says. We are not talking about mere repetition. We are referring specifically to a genuine emphatic conversational skill. The three central elements in successful conversation control are the skills of recognizing, appreciating and understanding what another person has said as a basis for your response.

At work things do not always go as we would like or plan. We find ourselves in situations with the potential for conflict. We are under pressure to produce against deadlines. We have to work with people who have different priorities to ourselves. All these are typical situations where conversation control is vital, and in particular the summarizing skill is a key factor in success or failure. We shall look at an example as we discuss the value of summarizing as an integral part of our conversation control skills.

## THE PROBLEM
Take the case of a marketing manager whose boss, the general manager, said 'We will need to bring forward the date of your report on Marketing Strategy by a month. I am under pressure from Head Office to get all our plans in quickly'.

If the marketing manager knows that the report cannot be completed in that time, he needs to be able to state his position in order to get a solution that will be acceptable to both parties. The way he controls the conversation will determine whether he has an argument or a problem-solving discussion with the general manager.

## POSSIBLE RESPONSES
What do you think would happen if he replied by starting off in any of the following ways?

- 'That's impossible. We can't possibly get through all that work if we have one month less in which to do it.'

- 'Look, if you told me at the beginning that we only had 2 months instead of 3, I could possibly have done something, but now we're committed to the existing timetable.'

- 'I give in. How can I hope to manage anything if you keep changing the deadlines?'

- 'Bringing the date forward by a month is so damned stupid! We will never be able to complete the project in that time.'

The question is, will these kinds of responses set the scene for a problem-solving debate, or a win/lose argument?

## HOW EACH PERSON SEES IT

The marketing manager feels very strongly that he has been put in a difficult situation. He has talked over with his own team the set plan, knowing that it will work according to the timetable. Now he is being asked at a moment's notice to change all the arrangements. This will have a demotivating effect on his own team members and it will seem to them that he cannot represent them properly with senior management.

From his boss's position, however, it is equally difficult. He has been told that he has to attend a meeting a month earlier than originally planned and present the group's marketing plan. If he turns up without the document, it will seem that he is not capable of organizing his own team and getting results.

## WHAT HAPPENED?

Here is a dilemma that can only be resolved through sensible and effective conversational control. The alternative is a slanging match between the general manager and the marketing manager, in which each tries to score points by putting the other down. That is exactly what happened in this particular conversation, and the following exchanges took place:

**General Manager:** You should know that in this business, no deadlines are sacred. If Head Office needs to change the dates, then we have to respond as best we can.

**Marketing Manager:** That's the trouble with this organization. Nobody gives a thought for those people who actually have to do the work.

## THE NEXT STEP

The marketing manager feels demotivated and upset. What course should the general manager now pursue?

- reiterate that the job must be done one month earlier than planned
- defend Head Office and his role as the go-between
- seek to understand the concerns of the marketing manager

The person exercising conversation control would tend to choose the last course, since the previous conversation has been no more than an exchange of statements, a series of generalizations, and a set of negative feelings from the marketing manager. If the general manager had exercised conversation control towards a problem-solving approach, the following would have occurred:

- the conversation would have been more specific

- the two people would have begun to talk about themselves and what the implications of the decision to bring the date forward by one month would have meant

- the general manager would have sought to recognize, understand and appreciate the points raised by the marketing manager

## How to Get On-side with People – Understand before You Judge

People will not always agree with you. Why should they? Even when you come up with really good ideas, others will find some way of criticizing them. 'Yes, but . . .' they will say as they overlook the 95 per cent of the good things you say and pick on the 5 per cent where they can score a point or object.

So how do you respond to people who seem to be against you? The first thing is, don't assume they are trying to knock you down. Maybe they do have a genuine point to make, or a criticism that can improve your ideas. But, more importantly, you must control your conversation in such situations.

There are three key words to remember. They are 'recognize', 'understand' and 'appreciate'. Everyone likes to be recognized, understood and appreciated. Therefore when you get opposition, summarize what the other person says by initially saying something like 'I recognize you see this will add to the cost. The way we can tackle this is . . .' This is preferable to 'You are wrong about the costs. I can prove my system will work'.

You can also say 'I appreciate your concern about the costs and I acknowledge the figures you have provided. The projections I have made are based on . . .' Again, you do not attack. You, in effect, reward the other person by 'appreciating' what he/she has said and 'acknowledging' their contribution. Because you behave in what the other person sees as a 'reasonable' way, he/she feels obliged, in most cases, to be reasonable to you.

> **Three Key Words**
> - Recognize
> - Understand
> - Appreciate

## How to Recognize, Appreciate and Understand

These are key points in getting people 'on side' rather than having them 'off-side'.

When you *recognize* what someone says, it does not mean you agree with it. You do, however, indicate you have heard his/her point and taken it into account. However, be specific. Actually say you recognize the point, then show it by summarizing it accurately.

Everyone likes to be *appreciated*. It is a mark of respect. It must, however, be genuinely meant, even if you disagree with the person. So if you say 'I appreciate that . . .', you are giving the other person respect and this helps build good relations.

111

To *understand* someone means you have listened to them even if you differ in your views. To hold a problem-solving discussion let people know you understand them by summarizing their views accurately. Either do it by a request, such a 'Let me see if I understand . . .', or do it by a statement, such as 'My understanding of your position is . . .'

## Summarizing as the Key to Problem-solving

Let us therefore return to the general manager in our case. For the purposes of illustration we can identify how the conversation could have changed if the general manager had behaved in an appropriate way. In real life it is impossible to control someone else's conversation, but it is possible to control your own. Only by doing this can one hope to move towards problem-solving. In this case the general manager has a demotivated, potentially aggressive marketing manager from whom he needs to get help and he could say 'John, I can recognize that by bringing the date forward it creates all sorts of problems which will interfere with the production of the report'.

The general manager's first step is to indicate that he personally recognizes the difficulties he is putting the marketing manager under. In this way he seeks to move the conversation to a more personal and specific level. However, in doing this, one should *not* always expect the other person to respond in a co-operative way. Initially people may become even more annoyed and upset. This should be expected and not deflect you from your prime objective of facilitating a problem-solving discussion rather than an argument. Let's say that the marketing manager, in this example, reacts strongly to what the general manager says.

**Marketing Manager:** Interfere is exactly the problem. That report is not the only job my people are working on. I have allocated work so that we could do a top class job. This change just disrupts the whole system and makes it impossible for me to manage properly.

At this point the general manager could be tempted to give the marketing manager a lecture on priorities. He might, for example, say 'Well, that is as may be, but the most important job that we have at the moment is to get the marketing plan out for next year in time for Head Office to discuss it and allocate a budget'. This may or may not have the desired effect of getting the marketing manager to co-operate.

## SUMMARIZE FEELINGS AS WELL AS FACTS

However, another approach based on the principles of conversation control would be for the general manager to follow up the feelings expressed by the marketing manager, and, in particular, summarize some of the key words he used, which he sees as problems that have to be overcome. In effect the general manager could indicate that he *understands* the marketing manager's position. In doing this he will be picking up the cues and clues and showing the marketing manager that he *appreciates* his special problems. This is how he could do that:

**General Manager:** I can appreciate that you and your team have a lot of work and want to do a top class job in each area. I also understand that the change will disrupt the system. What are the particular areas that will be affected?

The general manager has indicated that he 'recognizes, understands and appreciates' the problems that the marketing manager has raised. He actually uses the particular words that the other person has spoken. *He is letting the other person know that he knows what is being said, and is suspending judgement on this.*

Therefore, rather than starting an argument by forcing statements on the other person, the general manager has tried to set the groundwork for a problem-solving discussion on specifics of what can be done in order to achieve the change required. After his summary therefore he asks the specific question in an open-ended manner. In short, he encourages the marketing manager to talk about the problems before they start discussing solutions, as discussed in our problem centred/ solution centred analysis (Chapter 3).

## LISTENING TO THE ISSUES

How would you assess what happens next?

**Marketing Manager:** There are three parts to the job, as you know, dealing with the economic analysis of our market, the market research studies on consumer opinions, and the implications for the budget. We have contracted out the market research studies, but everything else we are doing ourselves. At our last meeting our work was on schedule and we are due to have a meeting with the consultants doing the market research in a couple of days' time. I could ask the outside consultants to speed up their work but they will probably say that will mean they will not be able to conduct as many interviews. Either that, or we might have to pay an extra fee for bringing in more staff to get the job done in a quicker period. As far as my own team is concerned, the assessment of the economy could be done more quickly but as you will appreciate, by having less time, our information will not be as good as it could be.

The marketing manager is now at least considering some specific ways to get around the problem. The conversation has moved away from general feelings, in which the marketing manager talks about 'them' at Head Office, towards ways in which the problem can actually be tackled in order to meet the objectives as outlined by the general manager. The marketing manager's energy is now moving in a more positive direction as far as the general manager is concerned. The general manager must now reinforce the positive points and, where possible, give help and support.

**General Manager:** It would certainly be very helpful if you could persuade the external consultants to speed up their work. If necessary, we could make a special payment to them for completing the job ahead of time, taken from one of the administrative budgets rather than your own, up to 10 per cent of the original cost. Talk it over with them and let me know what you feel would be best. Regarding the economic assessment, I understand that it would not be as extensive as you would normally produce. I shall make this clear when I present the report. Now you mentioned other jobs which would be interrupted.

**Marketing Manager:** Well, we have quite a lot of work at the moment on a number of products, particularly on the writing of specific marketing plans and doing some investigations on prices of competitors. I get upset because the brand managers start putting a lot of pressure on me when we don't meet the timetable to which we have agreed, and my own team also gets very upset because it makes us look unprofessional.

## TAKING ACTION

Again the general manager has a specific problem-solving issue with which to deal. Rather than talking in general terms, the marketing manager refers specifically to the brand managers and his own team. The general manager, if he was exercising conversation control, would pick up these two points and seek to help. He can do this by posing a question rather than giving the specific solution, to enable the marketing manager to consider options rather than just saying yes or no.

**General Manager:** I can appreciate that the change will bring about pressure from the brand managers and also understand that your own team would feel that work is being disrupted. To what extent would it help if I said at the next managers' meeting that bringing forward the marketing plan by a month will create a number of alterations to the schedule and that the brand managers should discuss their priorities with you. Also, it may be useful if I summarize our conversation today in a note which I can send to you. If you felt it was appropriate, you could circulate it for your next team meeting, so that when you present the changes to your own staff, they can understand the wider context of the decisions.

**Marketing Manager:** I think those two points would be very useful.

**General Manager:** Well, let's meet again in a week's time to see how things are going and discuss any of the issues arising, and thanks for helping speed up the plan so that I can present it to Head Office.

This case is written to highlight how a manager can use the skills of summarizing as the basis for moving a conversation to a successful resolution. In this process he makes effective use of the three key principles of recognizing, appreciating and understanding the concerns of the other person in order to reach a common understanding. These are the practical skills of active listening that are so important in conversation control. It is no use being good at summarizing and recognizing, appreciating and understanding if you then do not follow up with the correct action. Here the general manager, having identified the problems, moved speedily to resolve them.

All summaries must of course be accurate both with respect to facts and feelings. Therefore do not bias your summary. Keep it to the point, for you are at this stage looking for the maximum agreement, not disagreement. It is only when you have indicated to the other person that you can accurately summarize his/her position as well as your own that you will be able to move forward to new ground and begin to solve problems.

# Guidelines

This case again shows the way in which conversation control can influence the way a discussion goes. It could have been an outright argument ending in a win/lose meeting.

1. However, the general manager, by picking up the clues offered by the marketing manager, was able to conduct a problem-solving discussion.

2. He used the three key principles of recognizing, understanding and appreciating in dealing with the problems raised by the marketing manager.

3. By summarizing accurately he enabled the conversation to move forward in a sequential manner, with persuasion and co-operation being the key behaviours.

4. He moved from requests to statements and ensured he dealt with past, present and future concerns.

5. He diverged and converged by opening up and closing down the conversation in order to bring about problem-solving.

6. His tone of voice and physical behaviour indicated that he really did recognize, understand and appreciate what the other person was saying.

If your voice and behaviour do not convey what you are saying, the other person will probably reply 'I don't think that you really understand at all'. At this point, rather than reacting aggressively towards the other person, it is important that you either summarize accurately what has been said, or ask the other person to restate once again the main concerns.

So, when in difficulty, summarize. The more you practise, the better you will get. Start with phrases such as:

(a) Let me see if I can outline the main points we have discussed.
(b) 'As I see it, the concerns you have are . . .'
(c) 'I feel it would be useful if we agreed on the key issues so far.'

If the other person feels your summary is inaccurate, then ask him/her to do it till you both agree.

The principles of recognizing, understanding and appreciating are important in situations where people have strong feelings and may be upset by what is happening. By themselves, these principles of course do not produce problem-solving. They need to be supported by emphatic listening for the cues and clues offered by the other person and a willingness to talk about them. Usually you must build upon the other principles that have been identified here, such as moving from the general to the specific, dealing with the facts and the feelings expressed, and being, above all, able to talk at a personal level.

Nevertheless the phrases:

I recognize
I understand
I appreciate

can be of considerable importance in producing the right environment and atmosphere to help resolve conflicts, and are an essential element in effective conversation control.

# Exercise

Without turning to the case study in this chapter, summarize below the key points that the marketing manager wanted his boss to recognize, understand and appreciate.

_____

_____

_____

# CHAPTER ELEVEN

# Conversational Seduction and how to Manage it

'A gossip is one who talks to you about others; a bore is one who talks to you about himself; and a brilliant conversationalist is one who talks to you about yourself.'

*Lisa Kirk*

---

How often in a conversation do you find that you end up talking about matters that are a waste of time? How often do you feel at the end of a meeting that the really important points you wanted to discuss have hardly been covered? If this happens to you, then you are being seduced. In short, you are engaging in behaviour which you did not intend to, whether it be pleasurable or just plain costly. You can with skill, control the conversation.

This chapter therefore outlines:

- what conversational seduction means

- how to control a conventional agenda

- the five levels of conversation

- the conversational parcel game

- the importance of leading and following skills

- the need to know and nice to know issues

---

## What Conversational Seduction Means

All conversations, whether they be business of social, have agendas. In most cases they are not formal agendas. Nevertheless, if you stand back and listen to what is being said you can usually detect a number of topics being raised.

It is important in any conversation that your own topics are dealt with in such a way that you leave the meeting satisfied. However, all too often I find that people feel cheated. They will leave meetings mumbling that their main issue was not addressed, or saying that the meeting was a waste of time. This usually means someone else controlled the meeting and agendas of importance to them were covered. This is one illustration of how conversational seduction occurs.

Therefore when you get into a discussion or meeting, have clearly in your head the items you want covered. Make sure your agenda is thoroughly talked through. Ensure you manage the time available rather than letting the minutes tick by until there is no opportunity for you. In this way you will be able to manage the conversation rather than be seduced.

## Controlling the Agenda

What do you mean by the control of the agenda? A straightforward simple example occurs each day in social conversation. You meet a person whom you have not seen for a while. The conversation may go like this:

**You:** Hullo, how are you?

**Him:** Very well.

**You:** Did you have a good holiday?

**Him:** We had beautiful weather. Incidentally, how is your wife?

Suddenly the agenda has changed. Already three subjects have been introduced – the health of the other person, their holiday weather, and your wife. All this happens within a period of about 10 seconds.

Conversational agendas can change very quickly. It is up to you to ensure your agenda times are covered. You do not have to be brusque or aggressive. Just indicate you want time to discuss matters of importance to you.

The first thing to learn to ensure your agenda is covered is to identify the five levels of communication. All conversations revolve around these five factors, which are as follows:

| | |
|---|---|
| *Me* | My views and needs |
| *You* | Your views and wants |
| *Us* | Our mutual needs and wants |
| *Them* | Other people not here at present |
| *Things* | Inanimate topics suich as machinery or the weather |

These five levels enable you to chart fairly quickly what is going on in a conversation. You will find that where there is a low level of risk-taking, people will invariably talk about 'them' and 'things'. It is safe enough to talk about the foremen or the operators or the salesmen when they are not present, as they cannot answer back; and if you talk about the production system, the machine or the product, it may be relevant but not too risky.

It is when we begin to talk about ourselves that conversations usually come alive. If I tell you how I really feel and you do the same, then this is usually getting to a deeper personal level. It gcts even deeper when we talk about us and how we see and react to each other.

Therefore in conversations be prepared to use the five levels to ensure the key issues are thrashed through. For example, I recently went shopping for a new video system. The salesman showed me five different types and indicated the main features and benefits. The whole emphasis was on things. I wanted to get his opinions and feelings as well as the facts. I therefore changed the level of discussion by asking 'If you were going to buy one, which would you choose?' The conversation took a different turn. He began to speak personally, man to man, rather than salesman to customer. By finding out how he felt I gained reliable information on how to make my decision.

When you are having a conversation therefore, identify the agenda items you wish to cover and the level at which you plan to gain or give information. I find in a lot of my consulting work people are very poor at gaining information on the personal level. I therefore spend time getting them to ask questions about what the other person says quite straightforwardly e.g. 'How will what you have been saying about the organizational changes affect you personally?' or 'In what way do you see the situation having an impact on you?' These questions change the level of conversation from the general 'them' and 'things' to the personal specific 'you'.

Equally you can control the conversation by making statements rather than requests. Here you can indicate clearly how you feel by saying 'We have discussed the pros and cons of the organizational change but I want

121

to tell you how I feel about it personally'. This is a clear cue that you wish to mark out a special area on the agenda. You should then follow this general statement by some specifics. If other people do not respond appropriately, tell them how you want them to behave. Let them know you want them to recognize, appreciate and understand.

Therefore, look closely at what level conversation takes place. Is it about things, other people not present, about all of us, about you or about me? Make sure that the conversation covers the levels that you want to cover as well as the topics.

# How to Play the Conversational Parcels Game

Because conversations move so quickly, we may, from time to time, lose the thread of what is being discussed and become seduced through either neglect or data overload. This is because of what I have called the conversational parcels game.

It is analogous to the game of 'pass the parcel', in which a group of people pass a parcel with many wrappings on it, and when the music stops, whoever holds the parcel undoes a wrapping until the music starts again. No one person is given much time to unwrap the parcel before the music starts again and they have to pass the parcel. The person holding the parcel when the last wrapping is removed is deemed the winner and gets the prize.

I feel many business conversations are played in a similar fashion. There is instead a conversational parcel. No one person is allowed very long to unwrap what they have to say before they are interrupted or someone changes the direction. In such situations it becomes difficult, if not impossible, to hold a sequential conversation, as everyone is competing for the agenda.

If this begins to happen, a useful technique is quickly to summarize what others have said before introducing your own conversational parcel. Otherwise it is likely to get lost as everyone competes for airspace. By summarizing, even if you are not the chairperson, you are recognizing what has been said and providing a base on which to build.

There is no guarantee you will succeed first time. Be prepared to have your parcel lost rather than unwrapped. Don't be daunted. Try again and again.

But remember to summarize. Remember to recognize, appreciate and understand. Remember to ask as well as tell. This is particularly important as you finish. Invite people to open your parcel by saying 'What do you think of that?' or by saying 'I propose this as a line of action and would like a seconder', or, if you wish to force the pace, saying that you 'will put your views into action, unless there are major objections'. All these actions are designed to get people to focus on your agenda item, to open up your parcel, and you are unlikely to be seduced by other people's agendas dictating the short period of time you have available.

# Learn how to Lead and Follow for Success

La Bruyere cleverly summed up a major aspect of conversation control when he said 'It is a great misfortune neither to have enough wit to talk well, nor enough judgement to be silent'. It is important to know when to talk and when to listen.

Therefore look at all conversations to see who is leading and who is following. People who are leading a conversation will often, though not always, make more statements, while people who are following in a conversation often tend to ask more questions and summarize more often.

Successful conversation depends on people being willing to take either a leading or following role. Let us look at some examples.

A clear illustration, which has happened to most of us, comes when we enter a new town and want to know the directions.

'I am looking for the Regent Hotel. Can you tell me which way to go?' (indicating a willingness to follow).

You take the first road on the left and go towards the park. You will see the hotel next to the park' (leading).

This is a simple illustration where one person is leading the conversation and the other following. In business discussions it can become more complex. Take a company that produces bedroom furniture to meet individual needs:

**Production Manager:** The information from your sales representatives is getting worse. This week alone we have had four specifications wrong. When we make up the final order it has to be right.

**Sales Manager:** I know that, and I have told the sales reps to measure everything three times before they send in the order. The problem is that your people can't read or count.

**Production Manager:** It's your blokes that can't write. Here, have a look at these order notes. My people have done the best they can.

**Sales Manager:** OK, the figures could be clearer, but your people should ask if they are not sure of the measurements.

Here the conversation is a succession of statements. It is becoming a competitive win/lose conversation. Both the production manager and the sales manager are intent on leading the conversation. Eventually the sales manager acknowledges the point made by the production manager that the figures could be clearer, but then tries to seize the initiative by telling the other group what to do. This no doubt will lead to a further argument. Let us replay that conversation with the sales manager willing to follow in a sequential way for a while.

# How to Follow, then Lead

**Production Manager:** The information from your sales representatives is getting worse. This week alone we have had four specifications wrong. When we make up the final order it has to be right.

**Sales Manager:** What specifically is the problem?

**Production Manager:** Well, we made up four orders as outlined on the sales sheets, but when we delivered them they did not fit.

**Sales Manager:** I insist the sales people measure the requirements three times, so why has a problem emerged?

**Production Manager:** As far as I can see it, the problem is that the sales people don't make their figures clear and my people misinterpret them.

**Sales Manager:** OK, let's change the system and have all figures typed up and checked by the sales reps before they go to production.

**Production Manager:** That will slow things down, but it will stop the mistakes.

In this repeat the sales manager avoids a direct confrontation by following the production manager's criticism in a problem-centred way. He asks questions and then takes the key points emerging as the basis for making a solution-centred statement. He thus makes a move to lead the conversation and gets the agreement of the production manager.

These are simple examples of what can be a complex set of exchanges in everyday life. Some people do not like to 'follow' and show irritation when they have to do so. They prefer to 'lead' and have people respond to them. This is fine when you know a lot more about operations than the other people. The higher you go in an organization, the more skilled you need to become in leading and following in order to ensure effective conversational control.

As seen from the above example, those who lead do not always do so by making statements. The really skilled person can control a conversation through questions. This is probably most easily seen at an interview or when a doctor conducts a diagnosis with a patient. The questions in such situations guide and direct the territory upon which the discussion takes place.

# Control through Questions

Of course it is easier for an interviewer or, for example, a doctor to control the conversation by questions when they have the power of a job or medical knowledge as a key lever to influence the other person. It is not always so easy in business. However, skilled questioning is a key way of influencing the direction of a conversation:

**Patient:** I have a pain in the stomach.

**Doctor:** How long have you had it?

**Patient:** Two days.

**Doctor:** Is it a pain or an ache?

**Patient:** A pain.

**Doctor:** Have you eaten anything unusual in the last two days?

**Patient:** No.

**Doctor:** Have you had this problem before?

125

**Patient:** No.

**Doctor:** Has the pain got worse since yesterday?

**Patient:** Yes.

This is a typical discussion between doctor and patient. So far the doctor has done nothing but ask questions. The questions are mainly close-ended, requiring factual answers, often of a yes/no variety. It is clear, however, that while the patient has information on the problem, it is the doctor who is exercising conversation control through the use of questions. The doctor leads the conversation from issue to issue and the patient follows.

However, there can be a point in the conversation when the doctor decides to open up the dialogue more and give the conversational lead to the patient. To do this he may ask 'How are you feeling now?' This is a more open-ended, diverging question and the patient, if he/she so wishes, can then introduce new data rather than just responding to factual questions. At his point the doctor is indicating that he is prepared to follow what the patient says rather than lead.

In all conversations there have to be people who lead and others who follow. The skill in conversation control is to identify when you should be leading and developing your views and when you should be following.

By identifying who should lead and who should follow you can

- use time more effectively
- get to the point more quickly
- allow those with expertise the time to contribute
- improve the problem-solving relationship.

# What is Nice and What is Needful

Some information will illuminate a problem while other information will just cloud the issue. You need to distinguish quickly what is relevant and irrelevant. Do not be seduced by irrelevant information.

Bank managers have to be good at distinguishing what is nice for them to know from what they need to know. Every day they have people asking for loans, and the information the hopeful borrowers give has been known to be bent, twisted, turned upside down or manipulated in various other ways. People will do all sorts of things for money. In particular they will try to manipulate a conversation. So you do not have to be a bank manager in order to benefit from conversation control.

It is one area of business in which you do not and must not allow yourself to be seduced. Therefore be aware of what you absolutely must know and distinguish that from what it is nice to know. In short, concentrate on the musts rather than the wants.

Too many business conversations go on too long because people get seduced by the nice to know items and the want to know issues. By all means make a detour, take an interest, listen carefully, but ensure you cover as the top priority the essentials. The 'must knows' must come first.

One way is to prepare in advance. Write down what you need to know. When I am looking for a new house, this is what I do. It helps me focus not only on what I must have in the house but also helps me control my conversation when it comes to negotiating. Therefore avoid conversational seduction. Distinguish your needs and musts.

# Guidelines

Seduction basically means that you end up doing something that you had not intended. Therefore you can be seduced in conversation and the methods outlined in this chapter show how to prevent it happening to you. Instead of being a victim of conversation you can learn how to control proceedings.

Know what you want to achieve and ensure those issues get covered. Beware when others bring in conversational parcels that are not related to your issues. Make sure time does not slip by so that over 80 per cent of the meeting concentrates on the issues that others put forward. Learn how to move from a following role to a leading role. Make sure your conversational parcel is opened and dealt with.

All conversations have agendas. To avoid seduction make sure you manage the available time:

(a) to find out what you require

(b) to put forward the views you hold.

There are five levels of conversation and you should practise asking questions and making statements at all levels. In any conversation you can talk about:

- yourself
- the other person
- all those present
- others not present
- things and objects

Develop the skill of moving between each level in order to achieve your purpose.

Conversational parcels are present in every conversation. It is your task to decide whether to open someone else's parcel or get your own opened. Do not let time defeat you. Use the skills of summarizing to put your parcel into the discussion. Get people to focus on it by direct questions.

Leading and following are also key aspects of conversation. Principles for when to lead and follow are:

(a) You should lead the conversation when you have specific knowledge and expertise that is required to solve the problem.

(b) You should lead the conversation when it is your role to give some structure and organization to the conversation.

(c) You should follow when you are required to provide content for an already structured conversation.

(d) You should follow in a conversation when you consider the other person has more experience and knowledge.

As Baltasar Gracian said, 'In conversation discretion is more important than eloquence'. And so it is if you do not intend to be conversationally seduced.

Finally, remember that in all conversations there are things that are nice to know and things you absolutely must know. Do not let them slip away or avoid the question. At the end of the day, if you do, you will find you have lost the advantage. Control the conversation, do not get seduced!

# Exercises

1.  What are the key things in conversation you can do to improve the way you lead or follow?

2.  What are the main things you have noted that lead you

(a) to be seduced in conversation?

_____

(b) to seduce others in conversation?

_____

CHAPTER TWELVE

# How to Challenge Assumptions and be Assertive

'A wise man reflects before he speaks: a fool speaks, and then reflects on what he has uttered.'

*French proverb*

It often takes courage to challenge the thinking of others. If someone has put forward a proposal, any questioning of the basic assumptions can be seen as criticism. However, without such conversation control major errors can occur. This chapter shows how to be assertive when it is necessary.

In doing so it covers:

- the importance of questioning assumptions
- how to be assertive
- when to be assertive
- skill practice

## Saying What you Mean

Having the courage of your convictions is an important aspect of conversation. There are times when you have to say what you know will not be popular. You may have to stand up for your rights, confront someone who is not factually correct, or speak out to challenge opinions being put forward. You can do this in an angry and aggressive way or in an assertive manner.

There is a fine line between these two. While it is important to say what you mean and to mean what you say, it needs to be done in a planned way if it is to have a long-term effect. It is easy to lose your temper and this may have a temporary affect. However, where you have to manage people over a period of time you will quickly turn them off by such tactics and they will find ways of combating them. Developing the skills of assertion is one way round this dilemma.

Equally, assertion is valuable when you need to challenge false or misleading assumptions. You can do this either by making a request such as 'What evidence do you have to support your views?' or by making a statement such as 'When you give those views without any evidence, I am reluctant to agree to the proposal'. It may sound as if this is very negative, but in the context of the decision being taken it can be very helpful.

## Disastrous Assumptions

A lot of business conversations go wrong because people make wrong assumptions. Assumptions are usually errors of omission. People do not ask the right questions or they may take information as given. It is invariably a failure of conversation control as much as anything else.

The best way to check assumptions is to do it openly and consciously.

It can be useful to say 'Before we proceed with this deal, let us list all the major assumptions we are making and see if the information we have clarifies the situation'.

Assumptions are not easily clarified. People often make up their minds and assume that certain situations prevail. There are many lessons from wartime where senior officers on both sides made gross assumptions rather than checking the facts. Field-Marshal Montgomery, for example, was told before the troops landed at Arnheim that the Germans had the area covered. He assumed it was a very limited cover and proceeded. He did not check the reports, and made false assumptions. The cost, as we know, in lost human life, was horrific. Similar assumptions were made by the Germans, particularly in their attack on the eastern front against the Russians.

How in the heat of battle or the speed of business do we stand back and check assumptions? There are other sad examples of the failure to question and consider despite the evidence available.

False assumptions can and do kill. The main cause of aeroplane crashes today is faulty teamwork among the crew. They make false assumptions and do not check them out. The world's worst aviation disaster occurred, it is alleged, because the captain of a Boeing 747 taking off the runway in bad visibility believed he had the right of way. As they moved forward, another Boeing 747 was on the runway. In the ensuing crash hundreds of people lost their lives because an assumption had not been checked.

Professor Norman Dixon (1984), who has made a special study of such incidents, reports on another assumption that spelt disaster. 'On 14th April, 1912, Edward Smith, Master of the *Titanic*, received a radio message warning of icebergs on the route ahead. Unabashed he pressed on at full speed driving his ship through the night at 22 knots until stopped from further progress by an iceberg. In the event, he killed himself and 1400 of those he tried to please.'

More recently we have seen the horror pictures of the Challenger Space Shuttle bursting into flames in January 1986, killing all seven astronauts. The investigations now show that warnings had been given by the engineers about the problems associated with some of the seals. However, the warnings were not passed to the top NASA administrators because people lower down the chain of command assumed everything would be all right. It would appear that the nuclear explosion at Chernobyl likewise was the result of human error and false assumptions being made in decisions.

Irving Janis, a noted behavioural scientist, looked at how major political and business decisions are taken. He came to the conclusion that there is a danger of 'group think' occurring. He cites the Bay of Pigs decision by President Kennedy and his cabinet as an example of where people went along with the prevailing wisdom rather than assert their doubts and concerns, which could have led to a different outcome.

## What Assertion Means

Assertion means standing up for what you want. It means expressing opposition. It means confrontation. It takes courage. Some find it harder than others because of their natural easy-going style and therefore more practice is required.

However, the aim should not be just to gain a win. The aim should be to solve the problem and get the best result. That is why assertion should not be synonymous with aggression.

To be assertive respond first of all by understanding and recognizing what the other person has said, and then be positive in putting forward what you want. For example, imagine you have a tenancy agreement with someone who is renting a property you own for a year. A month before the agreement is due to end the tenant leaves the property and says you can take the remaining rent from the bond money that is held in trust to cover any damage created by the tenant. You must, in such situations, be assertive. But first understand and recognize. 'I understand you will be leaving the property one month early and want to pay the rent from the bond money. I cannot agree to that as it breaks our agreement.' Now this puts your position clearly and assertively.

In short, use the three-line assertion message, in which:

(a) you understand and summarize

(b) you indicate your feelings

(c) you state your requirements and reason, if appropriate.

## ASSERT THE 'I' MESSAGE

For the past 2 years I have been leading a project with the pilots and flight engineers of a major airline to enable them to work more effectively as a team. When we asked the aircrew what they particularly wanted to improve upon, they mentioned interpersonal communication.

The reason is that it is often difficult under conditions of high workload with a plane travelling at hundreds of miles per hour to always influence others in a proper way – particularly, for example, if a junior first officer is flying with a senior pilot with, say, over 30 years' experience. How should a junior officer try to influence the captain if he feels a procedure is being neglected or operations being conducted in a non-professional manner that could endanger safety? Unfortunately in some airlines the first officer says little, and has to bite his tongue, because the captain has total authority and the second pilot is only there as an insurance policy.

However, in our work the airline was keen to get more co-operation on the flight deck, particularly in difficult circumstances. One of the key rules we proposed therefore was that in challenging each other's assumptions pilots should not directly criticize others but first indicate their own concerns.

We have trained the pilots to use the 'I' message, followed by the 'concerned' message. The co-pilot can assert his position without being critical of the captain by saying 'Captain, I have not heard our runway clearance', 'I am concerned about taking off in the poor visibility', or 'I would like to check for safety reasons with Air Traffic Control'.

If the captain ignores him or says 'It will be all right', then the co-pilot must reiterate his message again, and if necessary again, by saying 'I understand you feel it will be all right, but I am still concerned and for safety reasons prefer to check with Air Traffic Control'.

If you are persistent enough you will usually win through even though it may take time. However, you have done so without being aggressive or submissive.

As part of this work with my colleague Dr Dick McCann we developed an easy-to-use model which can be applied in any situation. It is illustrated in Figure 12.1, which is explained below:

*Aggressive.* Here you will seek to get your own way at the expense of the other person. This usually means a 'put-down' of that person in some verbal or non-verbal manner.

| Own needs first | AGGRESSIVE | ASSERTIVE |
|---|---|---|
| Other's needs first | SUBMISSIVE | SUPPORTIVE |
| | 'Put-downs' occur | No 'put-downs' occur |

FIGURE 12.1

*Assertive.* Here you will put your own needs first but do so in a way that tries not to 'put down' the other person. We have stressed the importance of the 'I' message and the need to be persistent in a reasonable way.

*Submissive.* Here you give way to other people's needs at the expense of your own. You are willing to submit rather than stand up for your rights. There may of course be reasons but the result is you put yourself down.

*Supportive.* Here you put other people's needs first but do not put them or yourself down in the process. You are willing to help and do so in a manner that ensures the needs of others are met while you are a positive participant in the process.

Therefore if you wish to challenge assumptions try to be assertive, not aggressive. If you are in a position where you are helping, develop a supportive (proactive) rather than a submissive (compliant) role.

136

# The Abilene Paradox

One of the amusing incidents arising from not challenging assumptions comes from Jerry Harvey (1974). He visited his in-laws in Abilene, a Texas town. It was very hot and the house had no air-conditioning. His father-in-law said 'Let's go to Abilene for dinner'. It was a 100-mile journey there and back in 40 degree heat. Everyone agreed that the trip was uncomfortable and everyone arrived home tired.

When Jerry asked if they had enjoyed the trip, his wife, her mother and her father said no and they had only agreed to go in order to please everyone else. On hearing this, Jerry said he only went along to fit in with their wishes.

So it transpired they had all done the opposite of what they had intended to do because no one had questioned the assumption. As a result Jerry Harvey called this 'The Abilene Paradox'. It is a salutary tale, supporting the ideas on 'groupthink' to which we have referred.

So make sure in your team you don't all go along to try and please each other. As Edridge Cleaver said, 'Too much agreement kills a good chat. It may also create major disasters if we do not assert our position'.

In day-to-day conversation we all need to assess and check on assumptions and indeed challenge others in an assertive way if we consider they are wrong. The key is the conversation control that we exercise in the way we communicate. One major way that has been identified is the assertive as opposed to the aggressive way.

# How to be Assertive

This is particularly difficult when you are in a situation, as in the above cases, where you are a subordinate in a strongly hierarchical environment. It is not always easy to put forward your views without being seen to undermine the authority of the senior person.

So what can you do? You can be assertive without being aggressive. You can indicate your position by:

(a) describing the situation     – observation

(b) indicating your feelings     – concern

(c) outlining the requirements – consequence

There is no guarantee that in any of the above cases skilful assertion would have saved all lives, but it might have led to the checking of the assumptions.

## AN EXAMPLE OF ASSERTION

Would the use of assertion by the subordinate officers on the *Titanic* have saved the lives of those who perished? Could a more assertive approach have saved the Challenger crew? We shall never know but it shows the need for developing assertive skills when you believe assumptions should be challenged.

Assertion normally comprises what is called the three-line assertive message. This enables you to confront the other person with your concern without being personally aggressive, but it is not easy and demands skilful conversation control. For example, you might say:

1. When you . . .

2. It annoys me . . .

3. Because I would like . . .

Here the person relates the behaviour that causes offence, says how he/she feels and then gives a reason. Note there are no such attributions as 'You are deliberately annoying me', there are no swear words, there are no put-downs of the other person. The emphasis is on indicating how you feel and thereby seeking to gain a positive rather than an aggressive response from the other person.

Such tactics will work if the other person sees your communication as reasonable, problem-solving and justified. However, don't expect that they will react favourably first time. You may need to repeat the message in the same controlled conversational way as before.

This is not to say that you should not at times be verbally aggressive with some people if that is the only language they understand. However, it is usually the act of last rather than first resort if you wish to maintain conversation control and a problem-solving relationship.

## When to be Assertive

Clearly you should only be assertive when

- you have certain rights that are being infringed

- you have information that contradicts or is in conflict with what another person has

- you have a strong opinion that you feel is being ignored or undermined

In short, if you are going to be assertive you need to have some basis upon which to support a case.

However, do not expect everyone to agree with you just because you have a right to be assertive. Indeed you should expect that when you do assert your position, then the other person will react against you rather than just agree or withdraw. Therefore be prepared for a counter-assertion or even verbal aggression.

In such situations you must continue with your assertive behaviour. Do not give up. Just reassess your original point. Do not be sidetracked or seduced into talking about such other matters as the excuses the other person puts up or the allegations he/she makes about you. Go back to your original point and assert what you want – always of course using the three-line assertive message where you understand, express your requirement and give the reason for doing so. If you keep getting rejections, then you have to work out other strategies, which will probably push you into win/lose arrangements.

It can be really difficult if, for example, you have to confront your boss or a member of your family. In such situations it must be important and you must be confident you are right.

# Guidelines

1.  When you feel a person is moving into action before checking assumptions, ask:

    (a)  What are the likely key problem areas?

    (b)  Where are you most vulnerable?

    (c)  What will happen if the proposed plan does not work?

2.  Try to hold a 'devil's advocate' session, where members of the group try deliberately and openly to find holes in the assumptions and plans of others. Harold Geneen, the Chairman of the American conglomerate AT and T, did this on a regular basis to ensure all

his managers were making decisions, wherever possible, on facts rather than assumptions.

3. Ask people directly what assumptions they are making and get them to indicate why they hold such assumptions.

4. Provide time in the decision-making procedure to check assumptions rather than rushing into decisions without doing so.

5. Use conversational control to indicate that by questioning another person's assumptions you are not criticizing them, but seeking to be supportive and helpful in thinking things through.

6. Be assertive and use the three-line assertive message to get your point across in an adult person-to-person way.

7. Do not be easily put off or seduced. Repeat your assertive requirements despite opposition.

8. Seek at all times to solve problems rather than just gain a personal win, by understanding what the other person says, even if you do not agree with it.

9. Challenge in a non-aggressive manner by asking for clarification, and listen in order to understand.

10. If you need to assert yourself, do so by talking about your concerns and reasons rather than by accusing others of error or 'putting them down' by name-calling and other means.

## Exercises

1. You bought a pair of running shoes 7 days ago. You note that there is a slight hole appearing at the front of the right running shoe, indicating the rubber sole is coming apart. You take the shoes back to the retailer who says 'You must have been kicking a ball or something to cause that and it's only fair wear and tear so we could not replace it'. What would you say in an assertive way to challenge this and get the problem solved?

_____

_____

_____

_____

2.  You arrive at an airport 1 hour before your flight is due. You booked the flight 5 days ago by telephone and said you would pay for the ticket by a charge card on arrival at the airport. As you ask for your ticket, the clerk says 'I'm sorry the flight is full. As you had not arrived or paid for your ticket, we had to reassign your seat to someone else'. There are no other flights to your destination which will get you there in time for an important meeting. What would you say in an assertive way?

    _____

    _____

    _____

    _____

3.  Your boss says he is proceeding to buy a new computer. You know he is taking a risk because all the investigations are not complete, and although the budget has been allocated, the head of computing has not been informed. As the cost is over $50,000, you feel you should be assertive. What would you say?

    _____

    _____

    _____

# CHAPTER THIRTEEN

# The Art of Giving Feedback

'People ask you for criticism but they only want praise.'

*Somerset Maugham*

---

What is the objective of giving personal feedback? Ideally it is to help people to improve their performance, but whenever we start to talk to others about their behaviour, we can be on difficult ground. There is a danger that whatever we say may be treated as negative criticism as opposed to constructive help. It is the way in which we phrase feedback which determines whether it is a negative comment or a positive one.

This chapter introduces therefore:

- examples of feedback

- how to relate to criticism as advice

- key principles of giving feedback

- personal approaches to giving and receiving advice

---

## Letting Others Know

We all from time to time have to let others know how we see their performance. It may come about as part of a formal appraisal process that exists in the organization or simply because someone comes and says 'What did you think of my report?' or 'How well did you think I made the speech at the conference?'

In our conversations we should be conscious of the way we exercise conversation control when giving feedback. It is not an easy task, for a word out of place can easily give offence. Therefore when you give feedback, to what extent do you help people improve their performance?

1.  Do I encourage people to talk openly and praise jobs well done?

2.  Do I consistently discourage others by criticizing their work?

The way to give personal feedback, whether it is requested by the other person or acquired through an appraisal system, is therefore important. It is one area where conversation control can make major differences to whether ill-feeling or problem-solving results.

How would you react to the following feedback comments if you were the recipient in each case? Assume the conversation had developed to the point where you have exchanged views with your manager on the factors influencing your work and he understands the situation:

1.  'Your performance over the last year has been poor. You have been too careless and negligent in your ways and have not paid enough attention to detail. You don't seem to be pulling your weight and your department is not up to the standard of others. I feel you are a bit lazy in your approach. Overall, I'm disappointed with your performance.'

2.  'I would like to describe how I see your performance over the last year so we can discuss areas for improvement. First of all, let me acknowledge that your department has had a heavy workload this year and you have had to do this with no increase in staff. Having said that, there are a number of areas that I would like you to concentrate on.

    'As I see it, there are three key areas – these are the timing of reports, the absentee rate in your department and your leadership style. A major problem for me has been that five of your departmental reports have come in after the time that we had agreed upon, and this had made it difficult when I had to report to the Executive Board and ask for a deferral. The second area is that I notice the absenteeism rate in your department is running at 15 per cent, which is three times the level of other departments. I would like you to get yours in line with theirs. The third area I mentioned is your leadership style. I know you like to run things informally but I need to see that you hold meetings with your staff on a regular basis and that I receive minutes of those meetings. Now I would like to take each one of these points and discuss how you feel we can make improvements.'

The question is, which of these is the most effective form of personal feedback ? It depends on how the individual in question reacts. However, it is obvious that the two forms of feedback are very different.

# How Feedback Can Differ

In the first example the senior manager is giving feedback which is very *general* in nature. He is also making judgements without giving any facts. He is making personal allegations, which we call *attribution*. He indicates that he feels that the subordinate is 'careless', 'negligent' and 'lazy' in his work. The whole tone of the feedback is negative and critical rather than constructive. Moreover, it is difficult for the subordinate to understand specifically what particular areas need to be improved.

The second approach is more detailed and specific. First of all, the manager outlines that he wants to give some feedback which will lead to improvement and therefore sets the tone of constructive criticism. He follows this up with specific descriptions of particular issues and gives factual detail to support these. Therefore the subordinate has received feedback on which he can, should he wish, do something to improve the situation.

In the first instance the manager resorts to name-calling. He may feel he is justified, particularly if the subordinate had been careless, negligent and lazy. However, does that approach lead to improvement?

The second approach concentrates on the facts. The manager restricts himself to describing the events and indicating standards he wants achieved. In real life he may not of course give all the information in one go as it is presented above but discuss one issue at a time before moving on.

Which of these two forms of feedback will lead to the most useful problem-solving discussion? The ultimate test is whether any improvement occurs. However, by using conversation control, it is possible to influence the tenor and direction of the feedback. A lot of work has gone into looking at how people can give personal feedback without giving offence or raising aggression or defensiveness. The following points may be found to be useful tips even though they be difficult to apply in practice.

# How to Convert Criticism into Advice

Advice and criticism are two sides of the same coin. Often when we give advice to others it is received as criticism. The other person sees this as an attack and either withdraws or counter-attacks. Therefore the way we phrase our advice and the tone of voice we use is important. Our advice, while being well intentioned, can come across as a 'put-down' rather than a supportive comment.

There are times when others are directly critical of you for not performing in the way they wish. Here you may feel the need to be defensive or want to attack. It may be the right course if you attack, but you may not get any further feedback if you do. Therefore, wherever possible, regard criticism as advice. In short, turn what can be a negative statement into a positive proposal. A good way to do this is to suspend judgement, summarize what the other person says and try to convert their negative criticism into a positive proposal for action.

First of all, look for good points. If people are doing things well, let them know. Indicate that you have observed what they have done and how they have done it. Describe what you see before you comment on it. For example, 'Jim, I have just read your report on our marketing plans for next year. It makes sense to me and I like the new material you have brought in on competitors' pricing'.

Where appropriate, ask people if they want feedback. You may, for example, be giving unsolicited help. Feedback is usually received better if it is requested. Of course you cannot wait for a request if the situation is urgent and critical. However, where this is not the case, ask people if they want to hear your views.

Let people know that you are going to give them feedback, and tell them your aim is to improve the work situation – not to have a go at them. Make the feedback factual, based on an actual situation rather than general observations. Put the feedback in a form of what future improvements are required rather than statements of what has gone wrong. Be supportive and constructive.

Listen to what the other person has to say. Take a problem-centred role. If they are full of excuses and apologies, convert these into positives by asking 'What can be done to overcome these problems?'

Often the best form of feedback is to facilitate a self-critique. By asking the right open-ended questions you can get the other person to give themselves feedback. So see if they can give themselves the messages before you do so. In that case you have really succeeded by delivering the feedback in the most effective way.

# How Do You Sound?

Most of us never hear or see ourselves as others do. It is, however, possible to do so by using tape- and video-recorders. For example, why not leave a tape-recorder on at one of your meetings so you can listen to what you said and how you said it? I would suggest you get the agreement of the others attending, just in case they are concerned.

You can learn a lot about the pace and tone of your delivery from such recordings. You then practise the points that you want to improve, such as slowing down or speeding up your delivery.

Likewise you can learn a lot by video-recording some of your meetings. It will seem artificial at first, but most people quickly forget the camera. You need to choose the right meeting (preferably one with your own team rather than a critical negotiation). One particular benefit is to have the video play back to the whole team as a team building exercise so everyone can comment on how they performed and learn to do things' better.

At such meetings it is important to focus on the process rather than the content – although the review can often improve the latter. Get the team to focus on such questions as:

(a) How well did we use the time?

(b) To what extent did we pick up people's cues and clues?

(c) Did we move between facts and opinions and vice versa?

(d) To what extent did we work well as a team?

This kind of event once in a while is a great way to get real-life feedback on individual as well as team performance. It is especially helpful to people who need to get particular messages, such as:

- too much interrupting
- not keeping to the point
- time-wasting

People can therefore get direct feedback and begin to adjust their behaviour without having to be told. Increasingly we need to make more use of modern technology in providing feedback in order to help improve performance.

## Feedback through Humour

In the old cathedral at Chester there is a prayer which captures the spirit of useful feedback. It says simply: 'Give me a sense of humour Lord. Give me the grace to see a joke, to get some happiness from life and to pass it on to other folk'.

## WORDS AND PHRASES THAT USUALLY ANNOY

You should have known better . . .

I can see no point in . . .

You must realize that . . .

I find it difficult to believe . . .

With respect . . .

You can't do that . . .

That's irrelevant . . .

Don't be stupid . . .

Please add other phrases that annoy you

_____

_____

_____

*Guidelines:*   Avoid absolutes unless you mean them

Avoid putting the other person down

Avoid superior sounding judgements

There is no doubt in my mind that humour is a major contributory factor to successful conversations and meetings. I have noticed many times at management meetings when serious subjects are being discussed how the atmosphere has been improved by the injection of spontaneous humour. It is not so much that people tell formal jokes, but more that they see a funny side to the issue under discussion or point that is being made and respond accordingly, in the process giving feedback as part of the humour expressed.

The matter would not normally be funny outside the context in which the particular comment was made. However, the effect of somebody making a humorous comment does break whatever tension is around and creates an atmosphere of goodwill. It usually includes the provision of feedback to an individual or the group.

In one group with which I was working the subject of how much the project would cost arose. The accountants, who were known as 'Beanie Counters', were asked for their views. They said they would need to study the matter but felt that the costs would be too high. Another member of the group immediately commented 'That's the trouble with you Beanie Counters, you know the price of everything and the value of nothing'. This brought a considerable amount of laughter around the table and was taken in good spirit because of the way in which the comment had been made. However, it can equally be seen how such a comment, if it had been made in a different way, could have upset relations between both individuals and departments.

It is probably true that humour has the effect of improving working relations between people, even if it does not contribute to solving any specific problem. In essence humour between members of a group establishes an espirit de corps and common understanding. Often in meetings humour takes the form of repartee, whereby each individual or group scores points indirectly by the comments it makes in a humorous way about others.

Therefore an important aspect is the feedback which people receive through humour. Rather than tell people directly that they are not performing well or up to expectations, the message can be conveyed through humour. In one group the production manager had not completed a job which the other members felt he should have done. One member of the group therefore commented: 'The problem with you people in production is that getting the product out gets in the way of doing the real work'. Again the comment was taken in good spirit but the message was clear.

If there are any formal jokes, they usually come before the meeting or afterwards. It is more spontaneous humour which pervades the actual meeting, and this form of humour is often more potent in terms of its feedback and valuable in terms of its contribution to good relations than formal jokes. As Alexander Pope said, in his *Thoughts on Various Subjects* in 1727, 'Wit in conversation is only a readiness of thought and a facility of expression or (in the midwive's phrase) a quiet conception and an easy delivery'.

However, humour in conversations can be used in a negative and detrimental way. We have all been in meetings where we have seen one person try to 'put down' another person or department by making fun of them. If this is done in a friendly way, then it is usually seen as part of the give-and-take of business operations. If, however, such humour is injected in a serious way, then it usually exacerbates the problems between individuals and groups.

It is difficult therefore to say that in order to facilitate good conversation control we should be humorous in conversations or managerial meetings. However, it is probably appropriate to say that if there is an amusing side to the issue under discussion, then from time to time it should be brought out so that it gives people an opportunity to see the lighter side of the job at hand.

# Action Points to Improve Your Feedback Skills

1. *Emphasize what you see and hear.* Make personal feedback wherever possible *descriptive* rather than evaluative. Describe your own observations without making judgements as to whether you see the facts as good or bad, and leave the individuals free to make their own assessment.

2. *Concentrate on particular points.* Make feedback *specific* rather than general. As we saw in the above examples, it is easier for someone to relate to particular issues rather than respond to general statements.

3. *Outline the positive points.* Try to make the feedback *constructive* rather than negative. People often give feedback in the form of telling people what *not* to do rather than helping them find out what should be done. There is a need to exercise conversation control in order to look for areas of improvement rather than just concentrating on what has gone wrong.

4. *Indicate what can and should be done.* Emphasize feedback which is *practical*, so that the receiver can do something about it. It is important to give a person a specific indication of ways to improve. It is little help to say that an employee's performance is good or bad. You need to suggest specific improvements in areas over which the employee has control.

5. *Build on what people want.* Try to give feedback that is *asked for* rather than imposed. In reality this is not always possible, as it is

necessary, in order to get improvements, to bring people's attention to certain areas. Where this happens, it is important to tell employees why you are giving feedback.

6.  *Choose your time*. Make sure your feedback is *timed* properly. Do not just say a few quick words in a corridor to someone about improving performance. Take time to explain the situation, so that the employee can understand what you mean and can discuss it with you.

7.  *Reach an agreement*. Make sure you come to an *agreement* as to what can be done, and clarify this in terms of specific times and dates, to which you will work by summarizing the key points.

## How to Receive Feedback

We have concentrated so far on the person who is giving the feedback. However, it is equally important if you are receiving it, that you exercise conversation control. The usual tendency, particularly if the feedback is critical of your performance, is to be defensive, if not aggressive. Here are some useful guidelines which may be helpful in receiving feedback.

1.  Take criticism as advice.

2.  Summarize the criticism accurately and succinctly.

3.  Lean forward while doing so.

4.  Smile at the appropriate point (usually when you start to speak) to show you are not angry at the criticism but are able to take it in a problem-solving way.

5.  Ask, where appropriate, for specific suggestions of ways to improve.

6.  Thank the person if you feel the criticism or advice has been helpful.

7.  Go out and practise in order to improve.

## Guidelines

These points will ensure that you respond positively to criticisms rather than negatively. You may feel, however, that the other person is unfairly criticizing you and you may need to react to this in order to stand up for your position. If this is so, then you need to develop the skills of assertion without being unnecessarily aggressive.

In summary, the giving and receiving of personal feedback is essential if we are to improve our performance. It is a major managerial skill demanding conversation control. With practice you can improve both the giving of constructive advice and also the receiving of criticisms.

# Exercises

1.  One of your subordinates, who is accountable for doing audit reports, has been reported to you by clients for being 'arrogant', 'highly critical', and 'upsetting staff'. You have looked into these comments from the departmental heads who made them. They say he is a very thorough auditor but annoys people by implying they are not doing their job. They also say he is negative – always saying what is wrong but not giving positive guidelines on how to improve. If you were to give your subordinate some feedback, what are the steps you would take?

    _____

    _____

    _____

2.  You are asked by a friend who is a chemist to comment on a paper he has written for the company magazine. It is far too technical for a general audience. It is also too long and does not have any news value or human interest. You feel he should have it rewritten so that the reader can identify with it. His research, on which the paper is based, has led to the production of a new chemical product that makes sterilization of instruments much safer. What would you say to him?

    _____

    _____

    _____

# CHAPTER FOURTEEN

# When are you Negative and When are you Positive?

'Criticism is never inhibited by ignorance.'

*Harold Macmillan*

---

To some people half a glass of water is half empty. To others it is half full. It is just a matter of perception. The way we perceive what other people are saying can determine how we respond. People bring with them to conversations particular attitudes which determine to a large extent what they say. This chapter therefore outlines:

- the way people communicate

- how to give good and bad news

- the value of being a positive thinker

- guidelines on how to present positively

---

## What Kind of Person Are You?

Some people are what I shall call 'negatives'. Their conversations are punctuated with such phrases as 'It's too difficult', 'It can't be done', 'It's too hard' or 'We've tried that and it doesn't work'. They may be correct in their comments, but if they do not go beyond 'difficulty stating', then conversation is going to come to a dead end.

Of course it may be a tactic in certain situations to be negative. For example, in negotiations, it is often appropriate at certain stages to 'stonewall' and not respond other than to put up a series of negative comments.

It is important, however, to recognize the value of negative conversation. I have sat in many meetings where people have rushed forward and made decisions without considering the difficulties and the problems. I once had a colleague who was renowned for his negative thinking. He was indeed super-critical at times. He could fire holes in an argument from a hundred paces. He was often seen by others as a bit of a 'killjoy'. He tended to look upon the dark side of any proposition and see things that either had gone wrong or could go wrong.

Left to himself he was not going to make too many decisions. However as a member of a team in which his skills were used appropriately, he could and did make important contributions. He was asked to cast a critical eye over details and invariably found loopholes, particularly on projects in which he had particular technical knowledge. It was often left to others to deal with the issues identified, but he was very good at picking out the problems that others did not see. Therefore negative thinking and contributions to conversation are not always inappropriate. The key skill in conversation control is to be able to pick them up and make them constructive.

This is of course where we see the value of a positive attitude towards conversation. Those who approach conversation with a positive attitude will always be looking for the way around problems. They will emphasize options, ideas, possibilities, alternatives, and be continually searching for what could be. To them the half-empty glass is half full and indeed could get fuller.

# Good News, Bad News

A case where lack of communication led to further problems came to light recently. It was a case where the good news was given to the exclusion of the bad news.

A manager in a manufacturing organization had been under heavy pressure to produce a particular item in order to meet an expanding market demand. Head Office therefore indicated that greater output was needed from the factory. The manager responded and achieved the target set, but in the process had major problems in labour turnover, as a number of people left, refusing to work under the pressure. In addition, costs increased and labour disputes became more frequent.

When the Head Office general manager came to the factory, he asked how the production process was going. The factory manager reported the 'good news' that production targets were being met and indicated that things were going well. However, he omitted to talk about the increasing costs, labour problems and the number of people who were leaving. The result was that the Head Office manager gained an impression that all was well. However, the seeds of a serious decline had been planted. Over the next 9 months the problems got worse and eventually Head Office removed the factory manager for not being able to achieve targets within cost and having industrial relations problems.

The factory manager should have been able to give the 'good news' while confronting the Head Office manager with the problems that were being created. This perhaps could have been done in the following way:

**Head Office Manager:** How are things going?

**Factory Manager:** We've done very well. Over the last 3 months we've met all the increased output targets.

**Head Office Manager:** I'm really pleased about that because the demand from our customers has been very high and the only way we could satisfy their requirements was to increase production from your factory.

**Factory Manager:** People here responded very well and we have all worked under tremendous pressure in order to succeed. Everyone has done a fine job and they deserve congratulations and recognition for their effort. However, if we are to continue with the high output demands we need to look at some of the management implications. For example, a number of people have felt that the workload has been too high and they have decided to seek work elsewhere, and of course we have had a few disputes due to the extra load. We therefore need to increase the workforce in relation to the increased output if we are to continue at this rate. This will mean rewriting our budgets because the costs inevitably will increase.

**Head Office Manager:** How have your costs gone over the last 3 months?

**Factory Manager:** In the short term the unit cost of production has increased with all the overtime work and the breakdown of machinery that we've had due to excess loading. However, I have prepared a plan which shows that if we kept up this pace, then we could maintain the existing unit cost structure providing we got more backup support, particularly in the maintenance area, and a bigger budget for the night shift.

In this way the factory manager is beginning to confront the issues in a problem-solving way. Rather than just giving 'good news' to the Head Office manager he is also telling him what needs to be done to maintain levels of production. He is accomplishing this without complaining or criticising, but by putting forward positive proposals which will enable the organization to succeed. It is easy to see how such a situation could lead to a negative dialogue about all the problems and difficulties and the Head Office manager going away with the impression of 'bad news'.

The way in which information is presented definitely influences people's perceptions. People tend to like to hear good news. On some occasions people give others, particularly their bosses, good news when they should really be presenting the facts of the situation as they are and looking towards ways in which things can be improved. Such people are the optimists of conversation control. Their great strength in conversation is to give hope. At times their positive thinking may outrun the facts and indeed the possibilities. They are usually good at seeing the positive possibilities but ignore the dark side of things that could go wrong.

Beware of situations where people tell you what they think you want to hear. Find out the bad news as well as the good. It is best to hear it early rather than have to clear up a larger mess later on.

# Positive Thinking

There are times when not everything is going to plan. It is then you need to look for the positive line of thinking. I went to a meeting recently where the senior manager came in and told the group that a major contract, which they had been hoping to get, had been delayed for at least 3 months. This would set back the organization and the morale of everyone, as a number of jobs were dependent upon this particular contract. There was no escaping the fact that the delay in the signing of the contract was a major difficulty. However, rather than dwell upon the negative aspects, the senior manager presented the problem in a most positive way by exercising conversation control. He started in the following way:

'We were informed on Friday that our client has postponed the contract for the supply of materials from our organization. This contract is vital to us in order to maintain our levels of employment as well as meeting the budget that we have set ourselves. Let us therefore concentrate in this meeting on how we can secure that contract. To do that I want us to identify the issues that we must tackle over the next 3 months. Let us consider who we should talk to and how we should go about it. We can then assign responsibilities to individuals and get on with the job.'

Right from the beginning the senior manager was taking a positive attitude by tackling the problem rather than wallowing in the difficulties. He could have started the meeting by having everyone talk about the problems they confronted as a result of the delay in the contract and the possibility of not signing it in 3 months. However, by posing the problem in a positive rather than a negative way the senior manager got people thinking about what could be done. In essence, although the situation was one of bad news, he encouraged people to discuss how they could work to bring about good news. It is vital, if you wish to get people motivated and enthusiastic, to start by indicating something useful and positive can be done. It is the way in which you, as a member of the team, phrase your words and put your arguments that can influence people, either in a positive or negative direction.

It is important for people in managerial situations to strike the balance between good and bad news, and to control others' conversations so that they do the same.


## Look for 'More of' and Avoid the 'Lack of'

The way we phrase things is critical to the way people react. In my consulting work with various organisations I have been interested in how people put forward problems and the responses they get from others in solving them.

I have had the opportunity to read many consulting reports which have been supplied to organizations. Because consultants are only invited by the organization when there is a problem or issue to be confronted, there is a danger that the consultants only see the dark side. This is reflected not only in their written reports but in their conversations.

For example, in organizations I have seen people talk to members and then report back on what they have found. Usually the report back is a litany of difficulties that need to be rectified and these difficulties are stated as barriers and problems rather than challenges. For example, consultants will report back either in writing or in conversation using phrases such as:

- there is a lack of communication between departments

- there is a lack of motivation amongst junior staff

- there seems to be an absence of support for the planning initiatives taken

- there is a problem with decision-making

- training programmes are both inadequate and deficient

All these points may be correct. However, in expressing them in the above way we are reinforcing the difficulties rather than looking at ways of tackling them positively.


## How to Present Positively

An alternative way to put the points is as follows:

- there is an opportunity to improve communication between departments

- there is a need to develop motivation amongst junior staff

- it is proposed that support be given to the planning initiatives taken

- many people expressed the need to speed up decision-making

The change of phraseology may seem a small point, but in psychological terms it means that one is moving from emphasizing a difficulty to proposing a form of action. Of even greater importance it moves the situation way from a criticism to an area of improvement.

No one likes to feel that they have a lack of something or be accused of being inadequate in some shape or form. However, most people are prepared to concede that there is a need for improvement. Therefore in your conversation try to be more orientated towards improvement rather than indicating deficiencies. It is important to emphasize that things can get better rather than just pointing out that things are missing, lacking or in some way not right.

In doing this you will be seen as a positive rather than negative person. You conversation will move onwards rather than backwards. It will enable people to discuss what the improvements and developments can be rather than concentrating on what the deficiencies and problems are. In this way you will be able to guide the conversation towards resolutions and encourage others to contribute ideas. If we are to succeed, we must strive for developments, stop talking about what is lacking and concentrate on the need to improve.

# How To Manage Positives and Negatives

1. *Highlight achievements.* In giving good news *emphasize* the *facts* as they are and indicate to people what has been *achieved* or could be achieved within given periods.

2. *Provide a balanced view.* Do not paint 'a rosy picture' when the facts do not support such a conclusion. Give a *balanced view* of all the facts.

3. *Ask for cases.* When people are being negative in stating difficulties, ask them to give *specific examples* and ask them how such problems can be overcome.

4. *Indicate your feelings.* When an individual or group of people in a meeting is stating a lot of negatives, *state your feelings* about the tone of the conversation and at the same time write up all the negative points that have been made before asking how each could be tackled in a positive way.

5. *Clarify the implications.* Where people are being, in your view, *too positive* and *over-optimistic*, ask them to be specific on how they see their proposals being put into action with regard to time, cost and the allocation of work.

6. *Ask for ideas.* When you feel there is a need for positive contributions and they are lacking, it may be useful to stop the meeting and have a 'brainstorm' session in which you concentrate, without question or criticism, on *positive ideas* which can be evaluated later.

7. *Reward positive behaviour*. When people are being positive in a constructive purposeful fashion, reinforce and *reward their endeavour* through praise, and other means, to encourage them.

8. *Convert bad news to action options*. When presenting 'bad news', put it in such a way that people feel that they can actually *do something about it*, as did, for instance, the senior manager above who had to tell his staff about the contract which had not been signed.

9. *Present the facts*. When presenting a problem, let people have the *facts before your interpretation*, so that they can make their own judgements wherever that is approporiate.

10. *Forewarn people*. If you have to give 'bad news', *warn people in advance*. Tell them that you are about to give them 'bad news' before you actually deliver it, as people do not like surprises. This is particularly important if you are giving serious news to a person. For example, in the case of letting someone know about an accident that has occurred to a friend or relative, it is important that you say in advance 'I have some bad news to tell you . . .' This at least forewarns people and prepares them psychologically for something which they may find to be a shock to their system. Equally if you are giving 'good news' to someone, it is helpful if you let them know in advance, so that again they can be *psychologically prepared* for what you have to say.

# Guidelines

All communication has some element of 'good news' and 'bad news'. It is the way we present what we have to say that determines, to a large extent, how people act upon it. If we present things in a negative way, then we should not be surprised when people feel despondent and rather unmotivated to do anything about it. If, on the other hand, we present things in a more positive 'good news' style, then we can at least enable people to feel that there is something that can be done.

In business the object is to get things done. The job of managers is to exercise conversational control in such a way that they can motivate and influence people. The way in which managers handle the 'good news' and 'bad news' aspects of conversation is therefore central and critical to the way people perform at work.

Therefore you should help yourself and others to:

- convert negatives to positives

- emphasize the need for improvements rather than deficiencies

- seek opportunities but test for the barriers and difficulties

- reward effective behaviour

# Exercises

1.  The following is an example of negative communication that could occur on an aeroplane. After about 15 minutes the pilot speaks to you on the intercom as follows:

    'Good morning, this is your pilot speaking. We are going to have to delay our departure for about 40 minutes. There have been problems with the cargo operators loading the cargo onto the aeroplane and this will take time to sort out. The plane is also at the present time being refuelled so it is essential that there is no smoking because of the obvious dangers.

    'When we take off, we shall be flying due east and going to a height of 30,000 feet. The weather forecast in the area is not good and it looks as if we could have quite a bit of turbulence en route, so please keep in your seats and fasten your safety belts. I understand the weather in Maytown is also bad for this time of year. The forecast is for persistent rain, the temperature just above freezing.

    'I will let you know if we have any further information.'

    All the information that the captain gave was, as far as he was concerned, entirely correct. It was a factual description of the situation. However, has he presented the information in the best possible way?

    Essentially he has given news to the passengers in a negative form. He has told them that they would be 40 minutes late, that there would be turbulence en route, that there was a fire danger and that there

163

would be bad weather when they landed. All this was important information that the passengers needed to know. However, even before the flight had taken off, he had put the passengers in a poor psychological mood for the journey. If he had been exercising conversation control he would have tried to present the information in such a way that the passengers looked on it in a positive rather than a negative way.

Could you communicate this information in a positive way?

_____

_____

_____

2. Imagine you manage a group of twenty stores. It looks as if the loss for the year will be about £1 million. Each store has five major areas, namely furnishings, clothing, hardware, electrical and books. You feel the store managers need to put more effort into increasing sales. How could you manage this positively?

_____

_____

_____

_____

CHAPTER FIFTEEN

# How to Speed Up and Slow Down Conversations

'What we say in haste we live to regret at leisure.'

*Anon*

---

An important aspect of all conversations is the speed at which who says what to whom. Conversations can go either too slowly or too quickly. A skill of conversation control is to know when and how to speed up or slow down the conversation.

This chapter will concentrate upon:

- why conversations go slow and fast

- methods for slowing down and speeding up conversations

- how to manage conversational time and meetings

- implementing the principles for success

---

Conversations invariably start going out of control when the speed of the conversation increases. Then you do not have sufficient time to think through the meaning and implications of your responses. It is therefore important to know how and when to slow down a conversation.

## Slowing Conversations Down

Let us start with the ways in which you can slow down a conversation that you feel is getting out of control. Imagine you are in a meeting and the other person is giving you a lot of information and pressing for a solution.

You feel you have not got enough information to offer a solution, yet the other person is pressing hard. You feel the whole meeting is going forward too quickly and you want to slow down the proceedings. These are some of the problem-centred things that you can do to retrieve control.

1.  *Reflect*. You can reflect back to the other person your feeling that things are moving too quickly by saying 'I can see that you want me to come up with a solution, but I feel I don't have enough information on the problem at this stage'.

2.  *Summarize*. You can summarize the situation by saying 'Let me go over the main points we have covered so far . . .' This will enable you to test out your understanding and provide a basis for clarification.

3.  *Ask open questions*. You can extend your problem enquiry by asking open-ended questions so that the other person is encouraged to concentrate more on the problem rather than the solution.

4.  *Make specific requests*. You can make requests that focus more on what has happened in the past or is happening now rather than committing yourself to a future-based statement.

5.  *Move towards general enquiry*. You can convert the other person's factual statements into an enquiry about how he/she feels about the issue, or you can convert a person's feelings/statements into enquiries about the facts and evidence underlying the feelings.

All these skills can help slow down a conversation without in any way being seen to avoid the issue or change the direction of the conversation. By using these skills you should indicate to the other person your wish to understand, recognize and appreciate what he/she is saying so that you can respond appropriately.

# High-Speed Conversational Attack and Defence

When everyone is acting in a rational, problem-solving way the above methods are easier to use than when a person is emotional or upset. It is when people start to lose control of their feelings that conversation often speeds up and people say things that they may regret.

When feelings are running high, we have an inclination to judge evaluate and use strong language. This invariably has the effect of 'putting others down'.

For example, consider the following:

**Manager:** Did you send this letter out?

**Subordinate:** Yes, what's wrong with it?

**Manager:** (getting very angry): What's wrong with it! You sent it out without me seeing and agreeing to it, that is what's wrong.

**Subordinate:** I was using my initiative.

**Manager:** If that's an example, then don't use it any more. You've made commitments in that letter which we can't fulfil. Have you got no sense!

**Subordinate:** Yes, I have, and there is nothing wrong with that letter except you want to make all the decisions. You don't trust anyone.

The scene is set for a high pace win/lose conversation where both people will make allegations against each other, attack and defend, and in all probability little problem-solving will take place. Feelings will become more important than the facts.

However, in order to improve the situation it is usually necessary to slow down the conversation rather than continue to make statements and personal judgements. Maybe the subordinate could do this by saying 'I can understand that you feel annoyed that the letter went out without you seeing it. I have not committed us without further discussion and I have indicated that these are my first thoughts in the letter'. Alternatively the manager could slow things down by saying in an assertive way 'I get concerned when you send such letters out before I see them because it affects future negotiations'.

Both sides can then take a breath, say they understand each other, and then start the problem-solving process of putting things right. The direction needs to be changed from what has happened in the past to what is happening in the present and what will happen in the future.

## Why Do Conversations Go Too Fast?

Conversations usually start moving too fast because people:

- move to solution-centred behaviour when they should still be problem-centred

- continue to make statements when they should be making requests

- move to discuss the future before they have sufficiently discussed the past and present

- start judging, name-calling, putting the other down, rather than understanding, recognizing and appreciating

You can soon recognize a conversation that is going too quickly. People are usually interrupting each other, not listening, holding a parallel conversation or indicating that they feel uncomfortable with the direction and pace. The person who is skilled in conversation control will quickly pick up the cues and clues and provide an opportunity for people to slow things down to gain mutual understanding and problem-solving.

# Speeding up Conversations

There are times when you need to speed up the conversation. It may well be someone in a meeting is going over the same ground for the third or fourth time. It could be that the people present do not have many ideas and this is providing a sticking point. It could be that you are bored and want the other person to get to some new, interesting material. All these conditions require that the conversational speed increases.

What can you do to improve the speed? There are a variety of methods, but it is important to judge the relevance of each one to the situation you face.

(a) *Be direct*. First of all you can be fairly direct and indicate to people you want to move on to a new topic.

(b) *Summarize and link*. You can summarize what has gone and then make a linking statement or question by saying 'How does all that relate to the plan for the next six months?'

(c) *Personal implications*. You can ask others a personal question, such as 'What are the personal implications for us?'

(d) *Questions and statements*. You can change the speed unilaterally by asking people specific questions or making specific statements.

168

(e)  *New ideas*. You can raise the pace by asking for and contributing new ideas, perhaps in a structured form, such as a brainstorming meeting.

(f)  *Time deadlines*. You can make a structural move by indicating the conversation has to be completed by a fixed time.

All these methods can, at the right place and time, have a big effect on the pace of a conversation. Usually when a conversation is going slowly, the energy level of the participants is low. Energy level relates to people's interest in and willingness to contribute to the topic under discussion. Therefore, if you detect the energy level is low, you may comment on that and you try to discover the reason people feel the conversation is going too slowly.

# Manage the Time Dimension

It is not easy to increase the speed of conversation in a problem-solving manner. However, a person skilled in conversation control can do it by focusing particularly on the time dimensions. How long should you allow for discussing past and present issues before you get to the key future problem? The chairman of a meeting needs to read the time allocation carefully to ensure that people feel they have an adequate chance to get their point across without being unduly rushed, but equally the pace of the conversation is not allowed to lag and become tedious.

The management of conversational time is a key to all successful conversational control. Knowing how to slow down or speed up a conversation provides a way of managing such time.

It is usually clear when people feel they are being rushed. Besides actually saying 'I think we need more time to discuss this', they will give other cues and clues. This may manifest itself in the well known phrase, 'yes, but', which is a classic way in which people refuse to be moved at the pace of the other person. Very often people will not move on because they feel their point has not been taken on board or recognized. It is important therefore not only to summarize points verbally but also visually. The fact that a person's point is listed and therefore discussable can often help speed up the discussion process.

169

Conversation control is concerned with ensuring people communicate clearly to resolve problems and make the best of opportunities. If your conversation is not being managed, it will end up either going too slowly or too quickly. Rather than reacting to such situations you can learn how to influence not only the direction but the pace of conversations and to achieve the purpose set.

# How to Keep Conversations on Track and on Time

One of the reasons conversations get out of control is that people wander from the point. The discussion may start on a specific issue but it can easily drift if people do not manage both the content and the process of conversation. Sir Winston Churchill summed this up nicely, saying 'When the eagles are silent, the parrots begin to jabber'.

It is easy to lapse into an uncontrolled conversation where all sorts of marginal if not irrelevant matters are raised. It is at this point that time begins to slip away and the meeting begins to fail. In short, the process is not in line with the content.

How can you ensure that everyone keeps to the point. First of all you must set an example. Secondly, you must carefully draw attention to the need to keep to the point if the meeting begins to stray. In short, you have to pay as much attention to the process of the discussion as you do to the content, particularly in formal meetings.

There are various ways in which you can do this, using cues and clues as well as direct indications. Here are some tips that can be useful. Some are standard practice. Others come with experience of exercising conversation control.

## BEFORE THE MEETING
It is important to condition people as to the expectations and requirements for the meeting. This can be done in various ways.

1.  *Talk* to people and find out what they want to achieve at a meeting before it begins. I have lots of people who ring me up and ask me to attend meetings. I always try and find out what we intend to aim for at the meeting and who else will be there. Very often I find that we can resolve many of the issues on the telephone and therefore no formal meeting is necessary. However, where a meeting is required,

I look for an indication of what will be covered, when, how and in what time.

2. Send *papers* round before a meeting. This helps focus attention on the issues, and enables people to prepare their own notes and information. Also ask people to write down in 200 words what they want to discuss with you and send it to you before the meeting. It helps them clarify their thoughts and it will save your time.

3. Circulate the *agenda* in advance. Again people can see the issues to be covered and prepare.

## DURING THE MEETING

4. All the above is pre-work. However, once you start the meeting, you also need to *condition the members* as to the issues. Clearly if you have an agenda, you will refer to this. But it can be a useful point to ask members if there are any other items of importance not on the agenda they wish to raise. It is best to do this at the beginning of the meeting rather than leave it to the end when time has run out. You may otherwise have people who try to rush through the formal agenda so they can raise their issues.

5. I have found it helpful at the beginning of the meeting if I am the chairperson to *indicate the time available* and check with members they can allocate that time. At this point it is useful to say 'Given we have a limited time, it is important that we work to the agenda and give each item the attention it deserves'.

6. *Take the prepared papers as read* rather than have each person make a speech going over the same ground again. You will probably have to be specific and say to the members 'We have all had the opportunity to read the papers. I shall take it that we are aware of the content. If a paper requires a brief introduction I would ask you in the interests of completing all the business to sum up in two or three minutes so we can get on to discuss the main points'.

7. If you are in the chair you should then ensure the people discussing each item *keep to the point*. Encourage the debate by asking for views. However, if you feel someone is getting off the track, ask 'How does that relate to the main point?' or summarize and say 'Given our objective is to reduce costs, is this point central to the main issue?' Enquire how the discussion relates to the objective.

8. You may feel you need to *provide a link to the conversation* in order to keep it to the point. For example, a number of people will ramble on about the past. You may feel it important to get to what should happen next. A good link question would be 'Given what you have been saying about the past, what are the current and future implications'. In this way you can redirect the focus and time dynamics of the meeting.

9. There may come the time when you have to indicate that in your judgement the other person is not talking to the point. If questions fail and linking enquiries fail, then you may have to *restate the ground* by saying 'The main priority for this meeting is cost control. The present discussion I can understand is of importance but it is dealing with issues that we should raise at another meeting. Let us look specifically at the cost control issues'.

10. It is useful to *recognize* when someone makes a *relevant contribution* that aids the discussion. By saying that a particular contribution is helpful you will give a cue to others how you feel they should contribute.

11. Do not be afraid to *talk about the process issues* in the meeting. Use your reflective skills to get people to focus on the way the meeting is going. You might say 'I feel we are moving rather slowly' or 'I'm concerned that not everyone is giving their views on these issues'. This again will get the members to realize that the management of the conversation is being noted and guidance given.

12. Finally *use your summarizing skills* to the full. This is an invaluable way to ensure everyone knows their point has been registered. It also enables you to take stock of the situation before moving on.

When summarizing you may wish to move in any of the following ways:

- from past to present to future
- from problem-centred to solution-centred or vice versa
- from parallel to sequential conversation
- from facts to opinions or vice versa
- from one agenda item to another

In short, keeping to the point is a skill. If you fail to manage the conversation, then the conversation will manage you. As Emerson so rightly observed, 'Conversation is an art in which a man has all mankind for his competitors, for it is that which they are practising every day while they live'.

# Words and Reasons

Conversations can get bogged down over the use of specific words. From time to time in conversations it is therefore necessary to change the ground on which you are putting forward your case. You may realize your case is untenable, or the opposition is not going to agree. You may, however, realize there is a different way round the obstacle.

I was in a negotiation with a large company and the issue of principle arose. We were discussing a complex contract which I believed required a period of continuing service after the delivery of the product. I therefore proposed a retainer arrangement. This was rejected, although the principle of after-sales service was accepted but on a 'as and when required' basis. I decided therefore to get below the problem/solution-centred line. I asked 'If the task requires follow-up service as agreed, what problems does a retainer create'. 'Well', said the manager from the other organization, 'we cannot enter into retainers beyond a fixed sum of $500. We would have to call it something else that would be acceptable'.

The clue was obvious. We had to change the ground and start talking about the same thing with a new name. We agreed that 'an appraisal review' would be acceptable as a basis for getting the agreement of those people in the organization who had to see a specific task associated with a commitment of funds rather than a general statement of intent.

# Provide Time for Thinking

I was once chairing a meeting when one of the members got up and said that he would have to leave. I was a little surprised, as we still had a number of points to cover. I asked him if he would be returning. He replied 'No, I feel I need time to think about what has been said. There is no point in me taking in any more information at the moment until I have had time to organize my thoughts on what has been said already. With this he left.

After a couple of days I received an interesting memo, summing up his views on the key points that had been raised in the discussion, and indicating his proposals. I invited this person to discuss the memorandum, and we agreed to place it on the agenda for our next meeting, so that everyone could benefit from his thoughts.

This may be an unusual incident. However, it illustrated how some people need time to digest what has been said, before they can contribute to the discussion. Not everyone is capable of reacting immediately to ideas and views. Some people like to take them away and consider what the options are.

I understand this, because, when I am under pressure, I like to do the same. If I am buying a car or in a negotiation, I rarely like to commit myself. I prefer to go away and digest what has been said before making a reply. As Matthew Prior said, 'They never taste who always drink; they always talk who never think.'

I refer to this need for people to go away and collect their thoughts as conversational digestion. In short, they receive too much information in too short a space for them to think about it and make a confident response. They don't like to be rushed and then have to retract.

I had a boss who recognized this when it came to making major decisions. He would call a meeting and tell people that the aim at this time was *not* to make a decision but to consider particular points. He would then have a sharing of views and ideas before calling another meeting 2 weeks later. By this time people had had time to digest the material from the previous meeting, as well as gather further information. While my boss always set a firm date for the final decision, he was willing up to that time to hold a number of meetings to enable people to digest information and refine their ideas. In this way they were able to exercise conversational control, based upon the digestion and careful consideration of what had gone before.

Digestion time can be provided by scheduling meetings so there are breaks. Such breaks can be short. For example, a meeting starting at 9.00 am will often break for coffee or morning tea at 10.30 am and recommence say 20 minutes later. This gives people a chance to consider their views before formal discussion restarts. Then lunch provides another break for consideration, say at 12.30 pm, before the meeting restarts at 2.00 pm. Here the break points are short but allow time for ligestion. On other occasions you may need much longer and plan to break for a week or more before restarting.

However, on some occasions, such as when you are negotiating, you may not want to allow time for digestion and consideration. As part of your strategy you will want to keep the pressure on. In such situations you will seek to keep the meeting going until you get a resolution.

# Guidelines

Knowing how to speed up or slow down a conversation is a key skill. It can, like other conversational skills, be learnt. In essence the skill of conversational speed uses all the parts of conversation control. We have shown how you can slow down conversation by the appropriate use of:

- reflection

- enquiry

- summary

Equally you can speed up conversation when you have to by such methods as:

- link statements

- proposals

- directions

- summarizing

The use of these methods will enable you and others to speak to the point more often. So often conversations get bogged down over the meaning of words. We need therefore to be flexible in identifying when to change ground. It will not always solve a problem but can often be the way round one.

Unless it is a social conversation, people will expect you to get to the point and stick to the point. You can manage this in various ways, including:

- briefing people beforehand

- getting people to put their thoughts on paper before you talk

- setting time limits to the meeting

- identifying clear objectives and asking people if what they are talking about relates to the objectives

- picking up on key words

- reinforcing a person with a non-verbal if they are on the point

- raising the process issues when you feel things are not on the right wavelength.

## Exercises

1. What are the main ways of slowing down a conversation?

_____

_____

2. If you are a chairperson of a meeting and there are a lot of items on the agenda but only 75 minutes available, what would you say at the start of the meeting?

_____

_____

_____

# CHAPTER SIXTEEN

# The Key Rules of Conversation Control

> 'He is an eloquent man who can treat humble subjects with delicacy, lofty things impressively and moderate things temperately.'
>
> *Cicero*

---

Conversation, like any skill, can improve with practice. First of all it requires that you know what you are doing and then try out the various skills. In this chapter ten key points, emerging from the issues raised, are outlined as guidelines for skill development.

---

## Build on Your Strengths and Practise

The first point to make is that you should not try to change your style of conversation overnight. The way you presently manage has a number of very strong elements about it insofar as you have been able to succeed so far. Therefore you should be looking to the 10 or 20 per cent of your conversation that you could improve.

The second point to emphasize is that you should practise the new skills in low-risk situations until you are comfortable and confident that you know how to use them. A good opportunity might be in social discussions or in non-urgent work situations. The best way of all is to attend a conversation control workshop course, where you will have the opportunity to meet others who are also working on their skills in key areas of business.

Certainly if you begin to succeed, it is likely other people will recognize this and in various ways congratulate you. Do not be surprised when they indicate your meeting went very well or say that they found your contributions helpful. Accept it as normal rather than going into long explanations about your use of conversation control techniques. This will only make people suspicious. Instead thank people for their comments and accept their praise in a positive way. After all they would not say it if they did not feel that you had managed the conversation effectively.

You can also learn by watching the way other people manage conversations. Some people provide a model of how not to do it. They may use long words or not listen and end up by frustrating everyone around them. Equally there are people who provide excellent models of conversational control. They are able to speak to the point, understand what others say, recognize and build upon the contributions, so that you feel at the end of the meeting the time has been well used. You should watch what these people do and learn from them.

However, there are ten specific conversation control guidelines which you can adopt on a regular basis, and these have been outlined below as a summary of some of the key issues in this book.

## 1. LISTEN FOR THE CUES AND CLUES

It has been said that in modern conversation the first person to draw breath is declared the listener. Many a true word is, of course, spoken in jest. Therefore if you want to improve your conversation control skills start with listening. This is not, as is often assumed, a passive activity. It requires a great deal of action. It can indeed be quite tiring.

The first thing to do is to listen and watch for the cues and clues. As indicated, these are the key words and phrases that people give during conversation which indicate points of interest or concern. In particular listen very hard when people use the words 'I', 'me', or 'my'. Concentrate especially when they follow this up with an adjective which indicates a point of concern, showing that they are worried, annoyed, happy, dissatisfied, or whatever state they feel is of importance. In such situations do not change the topic of discussion.

It is here that you can use your reflective skills or your open-ended enquiry questions. In particular refer to the key cue and clue words that have actually been used. You will be surprised at what others have to say if they feel that you are sufficiently interested. At times they may tell you things you feel are embarrassing. Do not, however, flinch or appear in any way flustered or embarrassed. It will mean that you have exercised very good conversation control to the point where people trust you. You should respect that trust and help them solve their problem. Also watch for the signs and signals. Notice how people lean forward or sit back in their chairs. Observe what is meant by the movement of the hands, the eyes or the head. Very often more is said in this way through signs and signals than by direct specch.

## 2. HOW TO BE PROBLEM- AND SOLUTION-CENTRED

Listening is a key skill in all business matters but particularly when it comes to decision-making. Those who are skilled in conversation control will know how to move from being problem-centred to solution-centred and vice versa.

You should usually stay in the problem-centred area until people have sufficient understanding of the causes before moving off into suggesting solutions. While this is a general rule, it does not however always apply. There are occasions when it is appropriate to put forward a solution although one does not fully understand the problem, e.g. in medicine, where on occasion people have put forward effective solutions even though the cause of the problem was not known.

Your conversation control skills will be judged largely by the way in which you handle problem-centred and solution-centred conversation. In a managerial role particularly it is important to know how and when to move between the problem and the solution. The first step is to improve your skills in enquiry, reflection and diagnosis in order to build up your problem-centred skills, and then work on your solution-centred skills of proposing and directing. Skill in these areas will help you to manage not only the direction but the pace of conversation.

## 3. MANAGE YOUR CONVERSATIONAL TIME

Like everything else in life, time for conversation is limited. Most meetings have a fixed period of time. It is your job to ensure that you are able to get across your points and understand those made by others. Therefore do not let conversations get bogged down on just one dimension such as the past. Be sure you also deal with present and future issues.

To do this you need to know how to link conversation between one time dimension and another. Too often conversations fail because people spend far too much of their time discussing the past and never get to what is happening now or what should happen in the future. It is your job to ensure that the time dynamics of conversation are handled so that you cover both causes and consequences.

## 4. TAKE A PERSONAL INTEREST IN PERMISSIONS AND TERRITORY

All conversation requires certain permission in order for progress to be made. Be conscious of the permissions that other people are prepared to give you if you approach a conversation in the right way. Permission is a vital factor in conversation, and failure to get it can lead to serious problems, as we saw in the example of the aircraft crash.

If you are not getting the right level of permission to enter into certain territory, then do not give up. If asking questions does not succeed, then become more assertive, particularly if you need the right to enter certain territory to do your job or solve a problem.

## 5. SEEK THE WIN/WIN OPTION AS THE FIRST PRIORITY

Many conversations in the work environment will contain a large element of negotiation, and you will find people will be either moving against you, moving away from you or moving towards you. Where you want to establish a continuing relationship over a period of time, it is clearly important to set up the conversation so that, without compromising the best answer, there is a win/win element in it for both parties. Clearly this is not always possible, but as your first option look for the win/win before looking for the win/lose option.

## 6. MANAGE BOTH THE FACTS AND THE OPINIONS

All conversations are a mixture of facts and opinions. It is necessary to use both to resolve problems. However, we often allow one to dominate the other. Sometimes we have too many opinions with not enough facts and sometimes it is the other way round. Therefore where you have opinions, ask for facts and where you have a lot of facts, ask for opinions. Watch out for those who try to persuade you simply on the strength of their opinion. They may be right but it is best to take time and gather some facts before deciding. Equally beware of those who have the facts and the opinions but are negative, for they will usually end up providing data on what you cannot do rather than what you can do.

## 7. CONVERT THE VERBALS TO THE VISUALS

Wherever possible in the problem-solving process it is important to provide an opportunity for people to see as well as hear. You can speed up the conversational decision-making process by providing information in a visual form. This can be done by writing up key points in the discussion as it proceeds as well as the normal way of circulating papers before meetings and facilitating the exchange of views in a form that people can read. Therefore the more you can convert verbal discussion into a visual form, the more likely it is that there will be greater understanding and the problem-solving process will be speeded up. My view is that the best investment any manager can make to facilitate this is to acquire a whiteboard or flip-chart for their office and use it frequently.

## 8. GIVE ACCURATE SUMMARIES – UNDERSTAND BEFORE YOU JUDGE

Conversation, like machinery, needs a lubricant to keep it moving smoothly. One of the best ways in which to facilitate smooth and effective conversation is to summarize regularly and accurately. In this way you can get agreement as you proceed and people will recognize your skill in drawing the threads of complex debate together. It is important, however, to summarize in words that other people use rather than in your own words. In this way people will identify very closely with what is being said.

In addition let people know you recognize, understand and appreciate what they are saying. This does not mean to say you have to agree with them. Summarizing through recognizing, appreciating and understanding is an essential part of clarifying issues rather than agreeing them. However, you will find that the more you clarify, through summarizing, the easier it will become to reach a decision.

## 9. ASSERT YOURSELF

One of the major causes of accidents and problems is that people do not challenge false assumptions. There are numerous examples where major disasters have occurred even though people knew in advance that there was something wrong. The real fault was that those who had the information did not have sufficient confidence to challenge those who are in authority.

A key skill of conversation control is to be assertive without being aggressive. This means using the three-line assertive message to indicate what you are concerned about, why you are concerned about it and what the consequences are likely to be. Therefore if in doubt, not only ask but inform other people in an assertive manner what you want, when and how.

## 10. EMPHASIZE THE POSITIVES

If you analyse people's conversation, you will find a great deal of negative thinking. You will hear people saying 'We cannot do this' or 'That is not possible'. However, real achievements can make people think in a positive way. Therefore train yourself to think about the positive side and seek out ways in which things can be done. However, this approach needs to be grounded on hard evidence rather than starry-eyed optimism.

Relate to people in a positive way. If they are negative, ask for the facts on which they base their thinking. Reflect your concern at negative thinking. Try to get people thinking about 'how to' rather than 'how not to'.

# The Effect Conversations Have on Relationships

Three main outcomes can emerge from conversations, as shown in Figure 16.1. These fundamental influences were outlined by the

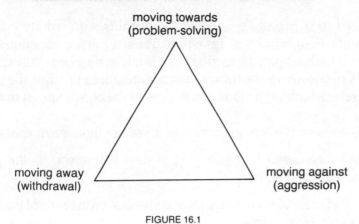

moving towards
(problem-solving)

moving away
(withdrawal)

moving against
(aggression)

FIGURE 16.1

psychoanalyst Karen Horney and indicate important responses that we all make, depending on how we feel a meeting has gone.

If the conversation has been a failure, you can expect people to withdraw either physically or maybe just verbally. They show a low inclination to follow your leads and indicate a low energy level.

If, however, people move against you and verbally attack, then clearly the conversation is not progressing in a problem-solving way. It may of course be necessary for them to lose their temper in order for progress to be made, insofar as people may only then take what they have to say seriously. However, in most cases hard words spoken aggressively make it difficult to reach agreement.

Moving towards each other in a co-operative approach is the best way to proceed in order to solve problems. This does not mean you have to agree with each other at every step. There will be differences of opinion, but with a professional approach through sound conversations, ask which of the three outcomes you want and then manage the conversation accordingly.

# Guidelines

All conversations require managing, otherwise they will go out of control. You need to keep your eye on what you are saying and how the other person responds within the time available. If you feel that time is being wasted, then seek to move the conversation forward. To do this you need to concentrate on what the outputs required are rather than the inputs. People in meetings will frequently put a tremendous amount of time into the inputs by talking a lot, but that may bear little relation to what is necessary in the form of outputs required to solve the problem.

Therefore look at the time dimension of the conversation in terms of:

- the amount of effort going into minor rather than major items

- examining carefully the amount of time you spend on the past, the present and the future

- looking particularly at the level of conversation in terms of the generalities and the specifics

- getting people to focus on speaking to the point

- mastering both how to slow down and speed up conversation at the appropriate time on the lines that we have discussed

Above all, keep your eye and ear on the objective you are trying to gain from the conversation, otherwise the conversation will control you rather than you control it.

These guidelines provide a quick overview and summary of some of the key issues that we have addressed in this book. Conversation control is a skill like any other managerial activity and can be developed and mastered. It is essential that we do so if we are to be more effective in the use of our time and in solving problems.

If all else fails we should heed the advice of Edward Hersey Richards who wrote:

> A wise old bird sat on an oak
> The more he saw the less he spoke
> The less he spoke the more he heard
> Why aren't we like that wise old bird?

# CHAPTER SEVENTEEN

# How You Can Use Conversation Control Skills

'Let thy speech be better than silence or be silent.'

*Dionysius the Elder*

---

The ideas outlined in this book can be used to improve the way we interact with other people. However, we need to practise the skills regularly. As with any other skill, performance will only improve with practice. At the beginning it will probably not be easy, but with regular effort you should see improvement in the way in which you relate with others and get things done. This chapter therefore concentrates on specific situations where you can:

- assess the way in which you relate with others at work

- review the way in which you relate with others in social situations

---

I spend a lot of time in my career working with managers who are responsible for achieving tasks and getting things done in organizations. When I ask them what are the major issues they have to overcome in order to get work done, they will invariably refer to communication problems between people. Many freely admit that they personally have problems communicating. They are usually clear on what they want, nor are they slow in putting into words what should happen. Their concern is that their communication does not have the desired affect.

Likewise many of the managers admit that they do not respond as positively as they might to other people's communication. They acknowledge, for example, that they are poor listeners and do not always find out what the other person is trying to say. Numerous managers have pointed out to me how this has led to poor decision-making, because key information has not been understood. This is why this book

185

on conversation control has been written. Therefore when we talk about managing conversations and improving conversation control, we are discussing the fundamental factors that make the difference between successful and unsuccessful business operations, which clearly can have a major effect on the profit and loss situation. However, beyond that and in the long term a more serious consequence is the effect that poor communication has on such matters as safety, productivity, personal motivation and other vital aspects affecting work life. We all know what it is like to be demotivated by someone who says the wrong thing. Likewise we have seen major industrial disputes erupt because of the lack of understanding and agreement between members of management and the shop-floor employees. Conversation control therefore is crucial to creating conditions where people work effectively together and gain job satisfaction as well as achieving the objectives.

Outside the workplace conversation control is equally important in terms of our social relations. The pace of modern life puts considerable strain on all of us as we rush from one activity to another. In the process the management of our personal relations can become strained, whether it be in the home or in social situations. Differences of opinion can lead to arguments and unpleasant conflicts or they can be sorted out through the skilful management of conversations. The aim of this book is to show the basic principles that you can use in order to achieve success in relations with others.

In my teaching work I am in contact on a regular basis with people who recognize the vital importance of conversational control in their job. I have outlined some of the areas within which the principles have been directly used and given examples of the important benefits and uses that have emerged.

## Managing Personal Problems

This is one of the most difficult areas in which to develop a successful conversation. If someone comes to you, whether it be at work or in social life, and says that he/she is having serious domestic problems, then you know that you need to handle the conversation skilfully, particularly if you are in a role relationship with that person such as a boss, colleague, friend, where there is an assumption that you will be able to help, not just in the short term but in the long term also.

If a man comes to you and says that his spouse, for example, has just left him and he does not know what to do, you may also wonder what you should do in the circumstances. Should you seek to withdraw from the conversation and suggest somebody else might help, or should you give him some advice as to how you would handle the situation.

Now these are only two options and readers of this book on conversational control will recognize that by applying the principles we should be getting below the problem-solving line to gather more information. We should be concentrating our efforts into a *problem-centred rather than a solution-centred* approach. In particular it is probably wise in the initial stages if we spend our time helping the other person to outline the problem and in this we must spend time reflecting his/her concerns.

A vital function in such a situation is to *understand without judging*. If we immediately rush in, indicating to other people that we think they are wrong, then they will probably cease to trust us. Equally we must avoid producing quick and facile solutions unless they be of short-term value to help overcome any immediate crisis.

Another important aspect of conversation control is to *get the individual to talk about himself/herself*. Where there is a personal crisis or difficulty, individuals may find it difficult to talk through what they consider to be the immediate problem. They may well look too much to the past and concentrate on what caused the problem. As we have found, one of the important principles is to get people to move from the past to the present and the future, and think about what their next steps will be rather than wallowing in the problems of yesterday. Therefore conversation control can be very valuable in dealing with some of the personal difficulties people bring to us from time, whether it be in the work situation or the home.

# Selecting New Colleagues

It has been said that you can tell what kind of a person anyone is by the company he/she keeps. The way we select our friends and colleagues therefore is vital. It is particularly important in terms of recruiting and selecting new people with whom we must work. If we make a mistake, it can have a serious impact upon relations at work, productivity and the success or failure of the enterprise.

I have learned from personal experience the long-term difficulties caused by selecting the wrong people. Invariably mistakes were made during interviewing in the way in which we conversed. On most occasions I and my colleagues who were doing the interviewing failed to get the correct information. We did not use the time dynamics well. We talked too much and the other person too little, and we ended up making the wrong choice. However, by looking at the way in which we use conversation control it is possible to be far more effective in our interviews and selection of people.

Naturally people when they are being interviewed want to make a good impression and put on their best face. I therefore now ask people to interact in various ways so that we can see how they come across in different situations. For example, I now ask the person who is applying for a senior management job to go round and interview a number of members of staff on a project. This enables me to see whether he/she is able to convince other colleagues by *asking the right questions* as well as being able to come back with views in a consulting capacity on the problem.

Applicants therefore have to show that they are skilled in conversation control both in *gaining information* as well as analysing it and *providing some ideas* on how to proceed. I also spend far more time in getting them to talk about themselves than about things.

I have also with my colleague, Dr Dick McCann, developed an instrument called the Team Management Index, which provides everyone who completes it with a 3000-word profile. We invite everyone who comes for selection to read the profile and then ask them whether they agree or disagree with it. Depending on what they say, we then ask them to give us examples and illustrations based on the items in the profile. This again enables us to centre the conversation on their interests, their perceptions, their experiences, and views, which are primarily what we want to hear. Therefore rather than conduct a direct interview, we provide situations and feedback to individuals upon which they can comment. All this makes it possible to generate information from people, so we can assess whether they fit into the work environment as we know it and they are provided with an opportunity to get to know us.

# Appraisal and Counselling

Over the last few years most large organizations have introduced the notion that people at all levels should receive an appraisal of their performance, and, where appropriate, be counselled on improvements.

Some managers find this easy, but most from my experience do not. They find it difficult to open up discussions with people on what could be weaknesses. There is often an assumption that such appraisals must start with criticism and this can of course lead to what we have described as the win–lose syndrome. We have the replay of 'Yes you did' 'No I didn't' conversation.

Most people recognize this sort of appraisal as not productive and try to avoid it. Many managers withdraw from such appraisal discussions and refuse to conduct them, but such behaviour is neither helpful to themselves nor to the people they should be appraising. I have found the reason people often avoid such appraisals is because they fear that the conversation will run out of control. The answer of course is to enable people to develop the conversation control skills to handle the meetings in a professional way.

Together with my colleagues I have spent a lot of time working with managers to develop their appraisal skills. The basic principles outlined in this book have been enormously helpful in giving people the confidence and insight into how they can manage situations. One of the first and most important issues of course is to get the persons who are being appraised to appraise themselves. The procedure is to get them to write down how they see their own performance over the period of time and to put this forward as the basis for discussion, thus enabling the manager to converse not on the basis of criticism but on the basis of giving advice. This is a very important strategic aspect as *criticism and advice are two sides of the same coin.*

In the appraisal and counselling process it has been important therefore to get managers to *look at the positives rather than the negatives* in a person's approach to work. I emphasize on occasions that managers should indicate to their subordinates and colleagues what they positively want them to do to improve rather than attack them for the things they fail to do. In short, I indicate what we want 'more of' rather than concentrating the conversation on what the person is 'lacking in'. This very simple change of emphasis makes a dramatic impact on the atmosphere of the conversation. People start looking for improvements rather than weaknesses.

# Managing Grievances

Another very difficult area for managers is the situation where people feel an injustice has been committed. Clearly in such situations people are aggrieved and there is a fair amount of ill-feeling. There is a danger that the conversation again can get out of control unless it is well managed. There are no golden rules, for this is an area which is invariably charged with emotion. However, as we have indicated earlier, one of the most important things you can do is to look at *the relation between facts and opinions*.

Where you have an opinion about a grievance, then ask for the facts which underly the point that is being made; likewise when you have a lot of facts about what has happened, ask for feelings and opinions about the matter. In this way you will begin to find that what may start as a slanging match can become a discussion if people really feel that you are prepared to *understand, recognize and appreciate* what they have to say. Throughout this book we have used those three words and emphasized how important it is to use them in a genuine and meaningful way. It is no use saying you want to understand, recognize and appreciate what people are saying when they have a grievance if you show with your body movements or follow-up comments that you really do not.

The starting point for handling a grievance must be to understand, recognize and appreciate; getting the facts and relating these to the opinions expressed; and allowing those who have the grievance to do the talking, so that they can see you are genuinely listening. After that, however, must come the application of the principles in relation to the facts and, where appropriate, a judgement must be made. Conversation control can make the management and handling of grievances effective and successful.

# Negotiation

A lot has been written on the different processes of negotiation with particular reference to the tactics of presenting an argument and seeking to win the case. A vital part of this is the way in which conversations are managed and controlled. The work done by Rackham and Morgan (1977) clearly indicated the importance of presenting one's case in such a way that it was discussable. Rackham and Morgan concluded that it was, for example, very important not to make attributions by labelling people with names, or implying that your case was fair and the other case was unfair. They termed these the 'irritators', which really upset other people and made them antagonistic towards one's own proposals.

They also indicated it was important to avoid constant interruptions and making counter-proposals when the other people were in the middle of putting their case. That led only to *'defend/attack'* spirals. The lessons of the authors' research indicate clearly that conversation control is vital if one is to become an effective negotiator. Such control comprises a thorough understanding of the *win–lose dynamics* to which we referred and an appreciation of how to manage the *continuum between rejection and acceptance*. Effective negotiators know *when to lead and when to follow*. They can appreciate the importance of respecting the other person's position without necessarily having to agree with it. Above all they recognize that there will be a tomorrow and the consequences of the decisions reached must anticipate the way in which people will behave as a result.

# Managing Meetings

When I ask people what it is that takes up the most time at work, they invariably tell me that it is attending meetings. Furthermore the thing which most often seems to frustrate people at work is not being able to get things done because they cannot get the agreement of people in these meetings. It is here that you need to exert the skills of conversation control in order to resolve matters within a particular time in an effective manner.

You will now be able to distinguish between a *parallel and a sequential conversation* and get people to talk on the same subject rather than many topics at the same time. Likewise it is important to allocate time in a meeting so that people can diverge and develop ideas on a problem before *converging* on particular options. Time dynamics are vitally important here to ensure that sufficient time is given both to the *diverging* and *converging*, to come up with some decision and action that people can accept.

Many meetings fail because those who are chairing them do not have the ability to *speed up or slow down* the conversation. This is another vital aspect of time dynamics which we have covered, and anyone who is responsible for a meeting should practise these skills in the context of conversational linking, which has been outlined. Here the chairperson can begin to condition and reinforce people's behaviour through a series of interventions designed to move people between *the past, the present and the future*. These conversational linking skills, which enable people

191

to look at *causes and consequences* within the framework, are very important. Continual practice, however, is needed, as one has to be looking at the process of the interaction between people as well as the content.

Most people who fail to run effective meetings become so intent on the *content* that they fail to spend enough time dealing with the *process* issues of territory, permissions in conversation, and all the other aspects that we have referred to. In this context it is particularly important to look at the *energy levels of people* who are in the meeting and see how they can best contribute. If there is a low level of energy, then give people an opportunity to contribute by asking *open-ended questions*, and how they feel about particular matters. It is equally important to ensure that people can contribute by enabling them to do the right preparation before they come to the meeting and having all the information so that sufficient thought can be given before discussion. It is these and other process matters that will facilitate a high level of effective discussion at meetings and enable people to use the time available to the best. Conversation control in this sense will produce the most effective decisions.

# Influencing Others

Every day in every meeting we are either being influenced or influencing others. We do this through conversation and various gestures. We have referred to the *cues and clues* and the *signs and signals* which are the basis of all interaction. We hope that the cues and the signs that we give to other people will be picked up and used appropriately; equally we need to be quick and accurate in identifying the clues and signals that other people give us and know how to respond. We have outlined various ways in which this can be done. It is important, for example, to listen to the *key words* used. In particular when they use the word 'me' or my, listen carefully for what they say next. Listen for the adjectives they use. Also listen for the point where people stop talking, for this is usually a strong clue because it indicates where you should either make a *request or a statement*.

Often we fall down in conversations because we make requests when we should make statements or we make statements when we should make requests. In a similar way we often fail to influence people because we offer solutions when we should be seeking to find the problem. Occasionally we try to find a problem when someone else wants us to give a solution.

## Summarizing and Asserting

It is not always easy to respond quickly but in conversation we usually have to. If we do not speak for about 2 or 3 seconds after the other person has finished, then they wonder whether in fact we are really interested. You must develop the skill of accurately *summarizing* what the other person has said, which will at least give you time to think, and perhaps the other person will also add some further information. Of all the skills of conversation control the one that needs to be practised most is that of accurate summaries which recognize, understand and appreciate what other people say.

However, in order to influence we also need to *challenge assumptions and assert* our position in a non-aggressive way when we have a legitimate case to put over. In many cases where people have failed to assert themselves, then situations of crisis have followed as we have evidenced with such situations as the sinking of the *Titanic*, the Chernobyl disaster and aviation crashes where doubt has existed before take-off. You will know of other situations from your own experience where there was a need for strong assertion to be made. However, we have differentiated this from aggressive behaviour, although at times it is often difficult not to be emotional when under stress and strain. In such situations it is important not to put down the other person but talk about your own concerns, doubts and what you want to achieve and why, so that people can understand the reasons behind you points.

## How Not to Use Conversation Control

A number of people have indicated to me that the ideas underlying conversation control can be misused. Conversation control skills are powerful tools which can be used to manipulate people. There is a difference between *influencing people and manipulating people*. I believe every day I and everyone else seek to have influence over others, but manipulation means taking unfair advantage of people. Conversation control therefore is not about controlling behaviour of others but getting control of our own conversation and behaviour. That is the prime aim, because trying to manipulate the conversation of others will invariably lead to a failure. People may not know exactly what you are doing, but they will sense that there is something wrong if you are trying to manipulate them. In such cases they will become resistant and *move away* or against you rather than *towards you*.

The aim of conversation control is to exercise discipline and skill upon yourself in the way in which you get information, use information and relate with others. If in doing so you control your own conversation so that you influence the others to behave in a problem-solving way, you have succeeded. People will look to see how congruent your words are with your actions. If they find there is a gap, then they will begin to suspect you do not really mean what you say, or say what you mean.

Therefore do not try to use the principles of conversation control for manipulation, but rather seek to apply them to yourself so that you can become more effective in the processes of influence and problem-solving. In that sense you will be seeking first to change your own approach rather than someone else's. If others see you performing more effectively, it is likely they will respond accordingly.

You will soon know whether or not you are effective because, as we indicated right at the beginning of the book, people will give you permission to go on to areas of their territory which they would otherwise have kept guarded. You will find that doors previously closed are opened. You will find that people will exhibit more trust in you and provide information and share ideas in a way that they did not do before.

## Guidelines

So if you want to know if you are really succeeding in conversation control, look at the way in which you are managing yourself and see what response you are getting from other people. If others are inviting you in to discuss matters, and sharing important information with you, then they are opening up personal territory and giving important permissions. This is a privilege only accorded to people they feel will respect what they are saying. When this happens on a regular basis with a wide variety of people, you can say that you are in charge of your own conversation control and that people recognize, understand and appreciate the way in which you respond to their clues and signals.

# CHAPTER EIGHTEEN

# How To Improve Your Conversation Control

'There's none so deaf as those that will not hear.'

*Matthew Henry*

---

In this final chapter you have the opportunity to develop action plans for improving your conversation control. This can be done in various ways and these are outlined.

---

In order to improve in any skill we need to gain feedback on how we perform. You may be exceptionally strong in certain areas of conversation control and in others capable of a much better performance. For example, you may feel that you are a poor listener but a good negotiator. Alternatively you may not feel at ease counselling someone on poor performance but enjoy selling a service or a product.

In our work as managers we have to engage in a wide range of conversation. We have to find out what is going on, analyse it, consider what should be done, make action choices and implement and review decisions. Somewhere along the line we shall have difficult conversations. This book has been designed to help you recognize why things go right and why they go wrong, and what you can do about them.

Therefore this chapter will be an opportunity to consider how you can improve. I have found checklists very helpful in guiding me to improved performance and I have therefore provided some which I hope may be useful. One of them comes from some feedback I gained from a group of managers.

195

# What Makes a Good Listener?

This is the question I asked senior managers on one of the managemen
development programmes I was teaching. I also asked them to indicat
what they felt were the characteristics of bad listeners and the result
below provide clear guidelines:

| Poor listeners | Good listeners |
|---|---|
| Interrupt | Patient |
| Change subject | Eye contact |
| Impetuous | Summarize to clarify |
| Inattentive | Put you at ease |
| Negative body language | Short prompts given |
| Easily distracted | Have empathy |
| Yes, but . . . people | Take time to listen |
| Impatient | Look attentive |
| Switch off | Ask open questions |
| Take over the conversation | Don't interrupt |
| Curt | Supportive body language |
| Thinking what they will say next | Show interest |
| Too talkative | Concentrate |
| Discouraging, e.g. look away | Ask about my feelings |
| Very critical | Pass few judgements |

There are therefore two ways to become a better listener. First cut out th
behaviours that annoy and switch others off. If you do interrupt a lot, the
exercise some discipline. If you do a lot of 'yes butting', then summariz
the other person's comment before you make your statement. If you d
have a defensive body posture, practise becoming more open.

Secondly, reinforce the things people like to see and hear in goo
listeners. Practise asking open questions and show interest in wha
others say.

As William Shakespeare said, it is important to 'Give every man thin
ear, but few thy voice. Take each man's censure, but reserve thy judge
ment'. This is still sound advice if you really want to find out what othe
think and feel.

The other side of the conversational coin is the skill of putting you
view across. Again I have asked managers what they regard as th
characteristics of effective and ineffective presenters, and these are som
of the major points to emerge:

| *Ineffective presenters* | *Effective presenters* |
| --- | --- |
| Vague – too general | Speak to the point |
| Exhibit lack of confidence | Illustrate with examples |
| Do not get to the point | Have the facts |
| Talk for themselves – not me | Address people's concerns |
| Poor eye contact | Open behaviour posture |
| Avoid questions | Respond well to questions |

There are other points which will be important to you but the above represent general pluses and minuses that people note when talking with others. It can make the difference to getting a job, losing an order, persuading a client, winning an argument, or a host of other conversational situations. So here are some ways you can go about improving your performance.

## Practise Your Listening and Presenting Skills

Until you know how you come across in meetings it is difficult to know what you have to improve. Therefore arrange for one of your meetings to be video-taped and then discuss the replay with a person who has some experience in human relations training and counselling.

Once you know what you want to do, set yourself a number of specific skills you wish to improve. Then systematically organize yourself to practise those skills. You can do this in various ways:

a) *Role playing* is a useful way of developing a skill. Here you simulate playing a particular part – such as selling a product, conducting a grievance interview or making a presentation. If done seriously, it can provide a great help.

b) *Real-life experiments* can be more risky but provide situations that count. In such trials it is best to try just a few skills at a time, such as asking open-ended questions or summarizing feelings before presentings.

c) *Case analysis* can be useful by observing other people demonstrate the skill you wish to improve. This is often called role modelling. It is the equivalent of watching a great golf player demonstrate the skill as

a basis for comparison. However, having seen the skill, it will tak
time to practise it to reach a high level of competence.

*Read and observe* what others are doing. There are now a number c
books on special skills such as selling and negotiating. This book wi]
provide most of the principles but you will do well to follow up witl
special books on particular skills and observe top performers if possibl
in the way they perform.

*Ask for feedback* when you feel others are in a position to commen
on what you are doing. At first people may be reluctant to tell you
particularly if they have a criticism. However, providing you give ther
permission and are not defensive, you will learn a lot.

*Watch how others react to you*, for this is really the acid test. Do the
move forward, away from or against you? Notice particularly the thing
you do that have a positive and a negative effect. The more you smile, as
open questions, provide accurate summaries and present views withou
putting others on the defensive, the more you will find people mov
toward you.

# How to Interact with Others

The studies that have been done show that the average manager spend
about three-quarters of every working week in conversation with other
It has been calculated that managers will be:

- listening for 45 per cent of their time

- talking for 30 per cent of their time

- reading for about 16 per cent of their time

- writing about 9 per cent of their time

Clearly these percentages change, depending on the level you are in th
managerial system and the nature of your job, whether it be in sale
research, personnel or other functions.

Therefore how we converse is a central factor in how successful we ar
in our job. It is no use being very able in terms of technical knowledg
unless you can influence and persuade others.

A key aspect of this is to know when you should be problem-centred and when to be solution-centred. As a key rule, it is wise if in doubt to 'get below the line' and be problem-centred before offering solutions.

Rudyard Kipling summed up the key skills for being problem-centred when he wrote 'I have six honest servants. They taught me all I know. Their names are, who, what, where, when, why and how'.

It is interesting to note that 'who, where and when' invariably lead to closed questions that require a specific factual or yes/no answer. In contrast, 'what, why and how' can usually be used to initiate an open question. Practice with these simple conversation starters can make a big difference in what you find out and the speed with which you do it.

# The Final Word is Yours

The essence of conversation control is that you take responsibility for what you say and how you say it. Conversation control is primarily controlling your own conversation in a skilful way, not manipulating others. It is appropriate therefore if you have the final word, and I have provided a short workbook where you can plan how you can further improve your conversation control skills.

Q1.   In your job what are the key conversation control skills required?

_____

_____

_____

_____

_____

Q2.  What are your key strengths when interacting with others?

_____

_____

_____

_____

Q3.  What are your key weaknesses in interacting with others?

_____

_____

_____

_____

Q4.  What can you do to improve your conversation control skills?

_____

_____

_____

_____

_____

25. How will you introduce conversation control skills to the colleagues in your team?

_____

_____

_____

_____

_____

26. In three months from now if you practise regularly, what results do you want to gain from using conversation control methods?

_____

_____

_____

_____

_____

# References

N. Dixon, 'Who Needs Enemies?', *British Psychological Association Bulletin*, November 1984, Vol. 37

H. Geneen and A. Moscow, *Managing*, Doubleday, 1984

J. Harvey, 'Managing Agreement in Organizations: the Abilene Paradox', *Organizational Dynamics*, Summer 1974

K. Horney, *The Neurotic Personality of Our Time*, New York: Norton, 1937

I. L. Janis, *Victims of Groupthink: psychological study of foreign policy decisions and fiascoes*, Boston: Houghton Mifflin, 1972

M. McPherson, *The Black Box*, Panther Granada Publishing, 1984

N. R. F. Maier, *Problem-Solving Discussions and Conferences*, McGraw-Hill, 1963.

C. J. Margerison and D. McCann, *The Team Management Index*, M.C.B. University Press, 1984.

C. J. Margerison, *How to Improve your Managerial Performance*, M.C.B. University Press, 1987

C. J. Margerison, *Managerial Problem Solving*, McGraw-Hill, 1974

N. Rackham and T. Morgan, *Behaviour Analysis in Training*, McGraw-Hill, 1977

N. Willis, 'Man of the Moment', *Personnel Management*, November 1984

# Index